We the Storytellers

We the Storytellers

Blending Our Stories with God's Story

Sally Armour Wotton

RESOURCE *Publications* · Eugene, Oregon

WE THE STORYTELLERS
Blending Our Stories with God's Story

Resource Publications
An Imprint of Wipf and Stock Publishers
199 W. 8th Ave., Suite 3
Eugene, OR 97401

www.wipfandstock.com

ISBN 13: 978-1-62032-535-2

Manufactured in the U.S.A.

To Mom, Ernest and Chris who are the inspiration and
substance of my sacred stories

Thanks To:

Bob Buckie, Hung Der, Maryn Madoff, Linda Peruzzi, Cordelia Strube, Christopher Taylor, and Amy Whitmore for their helpful feedback on Part One

Special thanks to Christopher Charles Wotton for his invaluable editing and advice.

Contents

PART 1

Our new
New Testament Stories

CHAPTER 1

Sacred Stories
Heal Us and Bring Us Home

Scripture Verses: Psalm 84:3 and Luke 5:17

We are a family with more books than can be found in some libraries, but reading is not only our preferred leisure activity; it is our soothing relief in times of stress. When our son Christopher was young and he scraped his knee or had a bad dream my husband, Ernest, or I read to him from a favorite book, often Winnie the Pooh.

However, one day I had no inclination to read. It was the day before I was to have eye surgery for a detached retina and there was a level of tension in the house that goes with a pending operation. I had been busy keeping busy, not wanting to think about the surgery when I noticed that our eight-year-old son's concerned questions had ceased. He was gone. I began to look around the apartment for him and my looking turned to searching. I had my hand on the phone to call

3

the neighbors when he stepped out of the large living-room closet. He said,

"Are you packed? I've got something important for you to take to the hospital 'cause you probably won't be able to read."

He handed me a cassette tape on which he had recorded our beloved Winnie the Pooh stories—stories that I could "read" in the hospital when my eye was bandaged.

That little tape is still my favorite book and just thinking of it brings me comfort whenever I "scrape my knee."

Since ancient times stories have been used to teach, preach and heal. The biblical narratives are full of such stories intermingled with our Christian history. These stories are effective because they don't judge or accuse individuals. They allow us to hear the truth about ourselves and our society through the actions of fictitious but authentic characters. They also affirm our best selves. These are sacred stories. This was Jesus' method of teaching and healing passed down to him from his Jewish culture.

Each of us has sacred stories that we have heard or experienced and they can heal or inspire us when we most need it. William Bausch, a writer and Roman Catholic theologian, defines sacred story as, "any story that contains an element of mystery and ends in hope."

The following story of home is, for me, a sacred story.

We were a contented family of three, I thought, when I was 5 years old. I rose early each morning and crawled into my parent's bed nestling into the warm space between them—taking my place as the center of the universe.

Then, without warning, to me, my parents divorced and my universe crumbled. My mother decided to move from our house in Springfield Illinois to Peoria, Illinois to be near her older sister, Clara, for comfort and support.

When Aunt Clara came to pick us up I grasped the wooden railing of the front porch of my home with all my five-year-old strength crying and howling at the top of my voice. This home was the symbol of my universe and I wasn't letting it go. It took both of the sisters to wrench me loose and get me into the car. Mom held me in her lap and wiped my tears throughout the eternity of that ride. She assured me that she could be both mother and father for me in our new home and through her love and determination she was.

Mom found an apartment at 171 North Street in Peoria, a hundred and fifty miles south of Chicago and a block and a half from Aunt Clara. 171 North Street became my home for the rest of my childhood and re-mains the symbol of home to me now.

Our apartment was in Miss Minnie Haley's early Victorian house. Miss Haley was also early Victorian. She wore rouge and lipstick every day which made her wrinkled face appear pink and white striped and she always bought dresses two sizes too large for her shrunken 85-year-old body believing they were just the right size: "In my day beautiful women were Rubenesque and my size has not changed." She had more space than income so was willing to have a little girl and her mother share her home. We had a separate apartment, of course, but I pretty much had the run of the house. The rooms had 14-foot high ceilings, marble fireplaces and ornate woodwork around the doors and windows. I loved the pocket doors between the old front and back parlors that slid in and out magically at my touch. But most of all I was fascinated by the newel post at the foot of the stairs. It had a non-functional, gas lamp rising up from it. This "lamp" was a tall brass pole threaded through a cylindrical piece of multi-colored cloisonné and topped with an etched glass shade. Half way up the stairs at the landing was a small ledge in front of a stained glass window—just the right size for me to sit and hold court, gazing down the long flight of stairs at my imaginary subjects and the majestic newel post. I sat in splendor dressed in Mother's velvet robe and pieces of her costume jewelry. At times I was a Queen (I felt princess was a menial role) or I was a bishop, depending on the daydream of the moment. I had seen bishops when the older kids at church were confirmed and they especially impressed me with their elegant costume and manner of authority.

The brick sidewalk leading up to the ginger bread trimmed front porch was the only pathway on the block that had not been replaced with concrete. The back garden began as a large, groomed lawn but paused at a hedge then continued on the other side as a half block area of trees, underbrush, wild flowers and snails. The other neighborhood children and I thought we were clever to call it the woods. When I grew up I learned it had been called that for generations.

By the time I was eight I had discovered the basement and it became exclusively my space. It was an unfinished basement just waiting for a child to decorate and furnish. There were, of course, high ceilings and the main room had wide planks, lain on the earth, that decades of basement floods had curled. When you walked across this floor, the metal tubs that held the coals for the furnace created a percussion symphony.

The other rooms in the basement had uncovered earth floors; the delicious musty smell permeated the whole space. I got all the cast offs from upstairs to furnish my underground haven; when the linoleum was replaced in our kitchen and when the stair carpet was renewed, I could put the old coverings down on my floor. I arranged garden furniture as a living room area, and leaned an old sink with 2 pipe legs under a wall faucet with a bucket under the drain to become my kitchen. The end of the room had a water heater with a little gas flame—the focus of my inventor's lab where I worked diligently on the plans for a robot and a flying carpet. The basement was not only my playhouse but also the neighborhood kid's meeting headquarters and center of fun. As its proprietor I was in charge and discovered a new way to be the center of the universe.

This was pre-Vatican Two and even with only two or three Roman Catholic families the neighborhood was overrun with children. I chose to befriend those who were two to four years younger than I which insured my authority and gave me the benefit of having "siblings" after school and quiet dreaming time in the evenings. In my basement, with my slightly younger followers, I was naturally Chief of Police or leading scientist, school principal or mother.

My friends and I "shopped" for groceries in the woods and had wonderful meals of mulberries and wild rhubarb. I dragged found objects home from the alley to use in my inventor's lab like interesting bottles, tire rims and the springs from an old car seat. My friend's parents wouldn't let such treasures into their homes but my basement playroom was my sanctuary and in it I was queen of the castle.

My aunt and the neighbors said, "Sally should be playing with children her own age, not playing let's pretend all the time down in that basement. How will she ever grow up?" But I believe the freedom my mother allowed me in my basement and my choice of friends gave me the confidence and leadership skills which as an only child I might not have gained.

When I reached teenaged years I outgrew a playroom, of course, but could still appreciate my basement haven as a retreat where I could dream and occasionally even do homework!

After University I moved to New York City and my mother joined me for only a few months before her death. She brought the piece of cloisonné from the newel post gas lamp with her because we knew the house was slated to be sold and then demolished.

The Christmas after Mother's death was bleak and lonely. All the decorating, gift-wrapping, eggnog and cheer among my friends just made me feel more alone. The New York I loved suddenly looked gray and withered and felt unresponsive. So, after many years away, I returned to Peoria to spend a few days around New Year's with old friends. There was a light fall of snow on the ground and after dinner one evening my friends drove me around town to see our childhood haunts. They thought that my old house had been demolished but I wanted to come home one last time. We arrived at 171 North Street after dark to find a cleared space where the house had been. The brick walk that had led up to the front porch was just visible under the thin blanket of snow—an eerie walk that led nowhere. I looked away, sheltering my home in my mind.

The house is gone but my home is indestructible. It is there in my taste for antiquity, and my love of wild spaces in the city, and in the occasional whiff of an earthy, musty scent. It is at the core of that sacred space in me where my independence, sense of freedom and creative imagination live.

CHAPTER 2

Aging
The Gift of a Lifetime

SCRIPTURE VERSES: JOB 12:12 AND 2 CORINTHIANS 4:16
AND MY FAVORITE, PSALM 92:14

I can no longer stretch the garment of middle age to fit me
and so must learn to wear my elder years with dignity.

I would like to think that as we age we gain a bit of
wisdom along with the wrinkles, aches and pains. Perhaps
gaining that wisdom is our reason for being. One definition
of wisdom is the ability to accept differences in one another,
difficult changes in our lives and ultimately to move into a
hopeful unknown.

We learn facts continually which introduce new
thoughts but our wisdom seems to come from our accumu-
lated life experiences, our relationships with others and the
evolution of self-knowledge. Ralph Richardson, the patri-
arch of 20th century theatre, said, at 80, "I'm just beginning
to get the hang of acting—of discovering who I am."

We humans may now reasonably expect to live a quarter, in many cases a third, of our lives after retirement. In some ways we can be our most productive in this third stage of life. As elders we become a rich resource of mature thought by reflecting on and sharing our own stories. We can identify those moments of wisdom that transform older into elder. We've all had mentors whose lives have shone a light in our lives and it can come as a pleasant surprise to realize that we are now someone else's mentor—what a gift! As with many, my mother was my most cherished mentor and I hope this story gives you a glimpse of her.

I still miss my mom even though she died over four decades ago when I had barely reached adulthood. A mental photo of when I last saw her is as clear to me as my fingers on this keyboard—her fine salt and pepper hair in a wave over her forehead, her still slender, stylishly dressed figure at 69 and that arched right eyebrow when she was bemused. I sometimes have fantasy tours with Mom around our technological world and imagine her particular mid-twentieth century reactions to my present lifestyle—cash from a cash machine, correspondence in cyber space, telephone conversations while walking down the street, Instant global access to anyone through Blog, Twitter or Facebook. I can put hundreds of books on what looks like her childhood chalk slate. To Mom a book had paper pages; a notebook was spiral bound, and a film spun into view on big, round reels.

She believed you could do any task needed in the kitchen with a table fork (and a strong mug of black coffee at your elbow— cappuccinos? I think not) and she didn't even drive a car; though there were cars when I was growing up! Her favorite mode of transportation was the taxi. When I was a little girl in Peoria, Illinois, I was not required to learn my address or phone number, my mother simply said,

"If you ever get lost just hail a cab and tell them you are Mrs. Armour's little girl and they will bring you home."

We didn't have a television when I was young.

"The radio and our imaginations," she said, "create much more vibrant pictures than anything shown on that box."

Little did either of us know the "boxes" that were still to come. We couldn't have imagined ipods, ipads or xboxes but we did go to the theatre, the movies and to baseball games every chance we got.

My mother had been the youngest of nine children with a weak body but a strong will. She was very bright and two years ahead of her age group through school—she told me she couldn't remember a year at her school desk without bricks under her feet. She graduated from university at a time when women usually didn't go to university. She had a lovely soprano voice in the church choir, taught school for several years and played bridge avidly. But in her forties, when she became a single parent of a five-year-old girl, other interests faded because the child came first. In fact, I do believe she postponed her death for my comfort and convenience.

I miss Mom but I haven't grieved her absence for a very long time. Instead, I remember the things she said and did that made her uniquely my mother and thoroughly enjoy her company in those memories. I was 6'2" by the age of twelve and she made sure I "knew" that being different was an asset, "I would rather be cheap than common" was one of her oft-repeated comments and she encouraged me to wear my height with pride. She was only 5'3" and one day when I refused to practice the piano she came into the room with a menacing look. When I stood up and she had to crane her neck to maintain that look, we both burst out laughing. The downside of that equitable relationship is that I still can't play the piano.

Mom needed to support us and had been away from teaching too long to take it up again easily so she talked an employer into hiring her as a receptionist / secretary with a schedule that matched my school hours and then taught herself how to type on the weekend before she started work. When not at work she used her remaining energy doing fun things with me—sometimes this meant the grocery shopping didn't get done and we dined on the food at hand. One day in health class we were each asked to detail what we had eaten for dinner the evening before. I was pleased to report, "A tin of smoked oysters, defrosted cupcakes and canned peas." I've had that meal since and still enjoy it.

My husband, Ernest, and I have a family photo gallery on the wall along the stairs and, naturally, it includes photos of my mother from her childhood to a picture taken in the last year of her life. These photos help to keep the physical side of her alive in my mind, but her love of reading, her style, her likes and dislikes make up the picture of her that shaped me and remains with me. I've tried to pass along a glimpse of this picture to Ernest and Chris, who never met her.

Over the decades I've traveled far from my life with Mom: to another country, another century, and, when I look in the mirror, I think another body. But from time to time I can sense her nearness, especially when I sip my black coffee or jump into a taxi or watch my son as he walks tall in his own unique way.

CHAPTER 3

Coming of Age
A Universal Dance

Scripture Verses: Philippians 4:13 and James 1:2

Growing up is not a Damascus Road experience, it is our human and individual evolution—a repeated event in a life-long journey. If we work at it we may come of age many times as we strive to become mature human beings. Perhaps maturing in mind and spirit is our prime responsibility in life— what life is all about. It involves risk-taking and a willingness to make mistakes, to regularly reinterpret our old "knowledge" and keep the wisdom of our mentors alive in our minds. As I continue my effort to become a grown up, I recall one of the early "coming of age" chapters in my life.

"We are the Cadillac of the dance industry," our manager, Mr. Hendricks, was fond of saying. I glanced around the studio with its worn floors and dingy wallpaper thinking we looked more like an old bike with a flat tire.

It was 1960 in Tulsa Oklahoma and jobs were scarce, particularly for me, a 19-year-old university drop out, away from home with absolutely no work experience. The newspaper ad stated, "No experience necessary, training provided." I thought, why not, I can dance, how hard can it be to teach it? They gave me six weeks of training, unpaid of course, and a starter roster of three students. I was required to see that those students renewed their contracts and to somehow acquire more students— from the inactive files, friends of the present students, the streets, wherever. But at least I was employed, albeit broke.

My first payday was two weeks away and salary advances were out of the question, but I headed up the stairs to Mr. Hendricks's office hoping he would make an exception.

Mr. Hendricks, or Bob as we were supposed to call him when students weren't around, was in. I tapped with my fingertips on the partially open door.

"Ahh . . . come in Sally, come in. My door is always open. You were miles away in the meeting today; we notice those things you know. It was a particularly important meeting too."

I eyed his enormous "Cadillac of the industry" oak desk and inhaled the fumes of his new broadloom.

"Well, I had sort of a headache this morning and ___"

"You're not quite coming along with the sales as we had hoped. Thought you wanted to be an actress. Well, selling contracts is your chance to practice. If you want to hear how it's done, listen in on James's renewal sessions, he's a pro, or better yet, Corrine's. I flipped on the intercom the other day during her interview with old Benson. It's her timing, you know. She came on to him, of course, not too much, just enough. Told him she couldn't get him out of her mind, mentioned her money problems and her insensitive husband—said the only thing that keeps her going is the thought of seeing him every Wednesday. I could hear he was eating it up."

"Yes but, well, the thing is Mr. Hendricks—Bob. . ."

"A while back she told a guy, who was determined not to renew, that if she didn't get another contract from him he could watch her jump out the third floor window right there and then. She had the tears, the whole bit. This is only her second year in the business and she's really raking it in. We give you the opportunity; it's up to you to get the commissions. Like I said in today's meeting: timing is all-important, when to put the screws in. It doesn't look like you're making enough to cover your dry cleaning. Your sales are gonna have to improve, you know, and soon."

I shrugged, nodded and backed out. I could feel my face burning as I thought of my earlier attempt at sales. Poor Mr. Romney. I sat him down in the little sales office and said, "The tango will change your life, Mr. Romney. The steps are a little tricky but once you master them your wife will be so thrilled she'll want a second honeymoon in Brazil." He burst into tears. How was I to know that his wife had just run off with a Spanish waiter taking his money, his car and his cocker spaniel? I felt so sorry for him I gave him my last twenty dollars. I'd never sell a contract; it just wasn't in me and I wondered why I had even considered approaching Mr. Hendricks for help.

However, I was a dreamer and had great hopes for my future. From the age of ten I'd known that I wanted to be an actress—not just a "performer" in California, but a real actress in New York. I felt destined for a higher purpose than "merely" housewife or businesswoman. I knew I was headed for New York City and a career in the theatre . . . eventually. But the more timid side of me whispered, "I've never even visited New York City; I don't feel ready for such a big step just yet." So, this first job would give me some experience coping on my own.

As I began to imagine decorating my own New York City apartment, an image of my mother came into my mind. Despite our more than usual age difference, she was in her forty's when I was born; I couldn't remember when she and I had not been each other's best friends. I could picture her now opening my most recent letter, her face lighting up when she read I'd found a job at last. Then I saw that right eyebrow of hers beginning to arch as she read what job I'd found. I could almost feel her thinking; "We had one of those dance studios in Peoria. The papers said it closed after the manager made off with the funds."

I wondered what she was telling my aunt and the neighbors when they asked about me. Probably something like, "She's . . . teaching dance" and then leave them with the impression I was giving tap lessons to under-privileged children. Mother's fertile imagination came to her aid in times of need. She had such confidence and went after her goals with little hesitation. She no doubt wondered why I thought I needed this Tulsa side trip on my way to Broadway. Mother would, of course, find some money for me if I asked, but she didn't have it to spare and though I couldn't imagine her saying it, I felt she would be disappointed in me if I asked for help. I sighed. "If I can't manage my life in Tulsa, how will I ever cope in New York City?"

The other dance instructors were all accomplished performers, almost acrobatic, but James stood out among them. He had the facial bone structure of a model, was slender and compact and could do four rotations on a spin. One and a half was my limit. My 6'2" frame, though shapely, could never get itself together to go in one direction longer than that. James's students were in awe of him, so grateful for the bit of glamour dancing with him gave to their lives, that they presented him with elaborate gifts—designer shirts, fine leather gloves, real gold cufflinks—all of which he accepted as his due. He and his student, Mrs. Dunkirk, twirled over to where I was standing and James introduced us.

"You both look wonderful in motion together," I said.

"Wait 'til you see young James in motion in the little two-seater convertible I'm giving him. We can dance all over town in that."

James looked genuinely surprised. His face took on a kind of Christmas morning glow as he waltzed Mrs. D. back into the ballroom to the refrains of number 17 on the sound system. Mrs. Dunkirk's floral patterned dress swung out as her step quickened and her nearly three hundred pounds actually seemed to float.

As the weeks went by, my dance skills improved but my sales technique did not. I tried calling the inactive files but they all gave me excuses for not renewing. I thought I'd convinced Mr. Bamberry to rejoin but then he began to talk about his asthma so I suggested he take up golf to add fresh air to his exercise . . . and he did. He thanked me profusely for the advice and asked me to remove his name from our files.

We were paid a base salary plus commission on our contract sales. The base salary would just about cover food and bus fare but not rent and clothing. Clothing is an important factor in the dance world, especially for the women. We were expected to wear a new, glamorous outfit every Friday to impress the students at the weekly afternoon party, or cotillion as it was called. I had borrowed money from James to pay the rent and was stretching my imagination to come up with ways to acquire fancy clothes.

It was Friday, the end of my third week, and cotillion day. I was free until second period so I stood and watched the others while the music eased me into my dream world. Daydreams had always played an important role in my life. They provided a world where I was the object of admiration and respect—where I could live up to being my mother's daughter. As waltz turned to tango my imagination swept the studio away and the faded ballroom became a Broadway theatre. In my fantasy I moved gracefully forward to deliver the impassioned speech that would end the act to thunderous applause.

As I took my imaginary bow, gold and green shoes glided into view and burst the bubble of my daydream.

It was break time and I made my way back to the lounge where the other instructors were getting coffee. I looked at the four of us women; a quarter to two in the afternoon and there we were in this scruffy little lounge, with its beat-up over stuffed furniture and ancient linoleum floor, drinking coffee from Styrofoam cups and wearing low cut satin dresses and high heeled shoes. I sipped my coffee carefully. Those cups had a tendency to leak. I envied Babette, a size two, her chiffon dress accentuating her delicacy. I considered myself slender at size 10 but felt like an overweight giraffe standing near her. And there was cherub faced Diane with her "naturally flat tummy"—I could tell she wore a girdle. Too bad James was not there. He was comfortable to be with and seemed genuinely interested in my, as yet, uneventful life. The others were fascinating to listen to— their lives filled with exotic travel and promiscuous sex, compared with my none-of-either. I was embarrassed to show my inexperience so I always joined the others in laughter or with a sage expression wondering all the while what they were talking about.

The break ended and like a school bell Corrine called out, "It's bird act time." Apparently, she had been a stripper years ago and her gimmick was a costume of feathers.

The slow, slow, quick, quick, slow of the fox trot greeted us as we opened the staff room door. We all followed Corrine into the ballroom, smiling and looking about for our students. Corrine's puffy, over-made-up eyes spotted her new student. She quickstepped up behind him, wrapped her arms around his middle and murmured, "This is our song, honey." The music changed from fox trot to jazz and Corrine broke into a solo. She was at least fifty, but boy could she dance.

I was booked with Mr. Humphries and the sucking sound of rubber gallowses being pulled from oxfords told me he had arrived. As usual, on Cotillion day the studio staff had filled the punch bowl, dimmed the lights and "formally" (over the loud speaker) invited the students to a ball. The male teachers all wore dark suits, white shirts and ties and each of us women were in four-inch heels, a glued-together hairstyle and yet another cocktail dress.

The wardrobe requirements were becoming a serious problem for me, so on this occasion I had carefully avoided the punch, smokers and anything that looked sticky. But I dropped my guard for just a moment. I should have seen it coming. Poor Mr. Humphries, a short man with a large head and thick graying hair couldn't walk (never mind dance) across the room without stumbling. He was headed my way with a cup of punch in each hand. He gestured for me to sit down and I felt the sudden sensation of icy cold wetness splash onto my cheek and for an instant numb my right shoulder. I watched in horror while the pale yellow satin of my dress turned burnt orange. The liquid ran down my right thigh and dripped off the hem onto my cream linen shoe.

Mr. Humphries stammered,

"Oh dear, I'm so sorry. That was typically clumsy of me. Let me get you another glass of punch or would you prefer a cookie or maybe a sit-down?"

"It's all right Mr. Humphries," I said. "I'll just nip into the staff room and dab these stains with soda water. You get yourself another glass of punch and I'll be back in a flash."

The stains were paler from the soda water wash, but were now stiff and definitely permanent. I had planned to take this dress back within the "I've changed my mind" time limit for a refund. . . but not now.

I returned to the ballroom to find Mr. Humphries chugging around in little circles with one of the new female students. With everyone dressed up and the dusty chandelier lights dimmed the ballroom was at its best. The old red velvet drapes pulled closed against the sunlight looked almost elegant. I watched the determination on the student's faces break into pure joy as a graceful move was accomplished.

The more experienced students were like extras on a movie set, swirling around in sound and motion. Even little Miss. Collier seemed to come out of her shyness on the dance floor, holding her head high and smiling directly at her partner and those she passed. When she waltzed her undulating movement was like a conductor's baton come to life and she seemed to know it. I had the feeling that the effort and expense were worth it to all of them because the weekly cotillions were their daydreams come true.

On the Monday morning of my fourth week as a dance instructor, I arrived at the studio to find a phone message in my box. A new student, I hoped, and blithely called the number. A young woman answered,

"Bandolf Finance, how can we help you?"

"Um, this is Sally Armour . . . you were calling?

"Just a moment." I heard a rustle of files. "We are representing The Ms. Susannah Dress Shoppe and it appears you have insufficiently funded them with a check, number 38, in the amount of one hundred and twenty three dollars and thirty seven cents. Bad checks of over fifty dollars are a federal offense, you know. But not to worry. We'll give you twenty four hours to make it good."

"Well you see the reason this happened ___"

I heard the click as she hung up the phone. I could hear, see, and feel my heart beating. Great. When I finally get to New York I'll have a record. If only I had learned to type or gained office clerk experience or something. Anything!

Thinking of my impending arrest, I reflected on how my mother handled difficult situations. When she was interviewed for a job she would answer, "Yes, I can do that" about any skills that were required. Then she would stay up for nights in a row reading manuals and teaching herself to type, crochet, drive a tractor—whatever. She believed that if anyone else could do a thing, that was proof that she could do it too. I wanted to be just like her, but I had had none of her brilliance when I was in school, and, as yet, none of her confidence, cleverness or wisdom. The only thing I was really good at was daydreaming and now, I thought, I'd probably end up going to jail. I guessed there would be plenty of time for my specialty there!

I arrived at the studio the next morning after a sleepless night. It was Tuesday, a Mr. Humphries' day, and he appeared punctually with a big smile as always. We began with the Magic Step (again) and I thought it would indeed be magic if he could execute it just once without stepping on my foot. We attempted a little spin— this man would never dance. From the corner of my eye I kept imagining a burly figure in an overcoat coming to hustle me down to the police station. I needed time for uninterrupted thought, so when the sound system developed hic-ups I nipped into the staff room. It was empty and quiet and I sank into the vinyl sofa. Again, a vision of my mother floated into my mind.

I could picture her sitting at the kitchen table, black coffee in hand. I knew she worried about how I was coping away from home. I breathed deeply and settled back into the sofa cushions, lulled by the hum of the little refrigerator. I began to imagine myself about six months hence on a plane flying to New York City. I smiled as I thought; others have had threatening financial difficulties and found a way to surmount them so I can too.

I went back out to the ballroom, moving in step with the rumba now playing. I sat down next to Mr. Humphries and listened to him as he told me how he was breaking in new shoes for this week's cotillion.

"I love this place," he said. "I never have been very good at meeting people but here it's so easy and everyone's so nice. I would never miss the Friday afternoon parties. I feel . . .I don't know. . . taller and well, really happy afterward. Even the punch is good!"

"Another six months of lessons would improve your dancing enormously," I lied. Then arching my right eyebrow slightly, I asked,

"Did you notice the way Miss. Collier was watching you at the last cotillion?"

I held a contract in my hand and he reached into his breast pocket for a pen.

CHAPTER 4

Does Risk, Perseverance and Justice Equal Faith?

SCRIPTURE: 1 TIMOTHY 4:16 AND JAMES 1:2–4 & 12

A definition of faith is a strong belief that something or someone is good, important, or valuable.

Certainly, Jesus was a risk taker and a perseverant seeker of justice. He stood up for his strong beliefs and he made enemies. That's the risk. But he was compassionate too and when it served his cause he was a diplomat so he also made friends and followers and became a model to live by for a large part of the world.

Most of us have conditioned ourselves to side-step controversy or risks and to avoid insulting those who might benefit us—it is less risky to flatter others or simply be noncommittal. To quote John F. Kennedy who was loosely quoting Edmund Burke: "For evil to triumph requires only that good men do nothing."

Often it is a child who will risk and find a solution to a challenging situation.

One spring Ernest and Chris and I made an urgent trip to London England to say goodbye to Ernest's mother who was dying. Chris was 6 years old but knew his only grandmother, Nana, from previous visits and could hardly wait to see her. She not only made his favorite pudding every time he came but she also told him about the toads in the back garden and the funny way Sandy Dog chased them and ran away from them at the same time. She didn't ask him dumb questions like, "How is school and did you like the food on the air plane?" She talked with him about things they both liked instead of just talking to the adults and she never pinched his cheeks or patted his head—he knew she loved him.

But when we arrived we found that Nana had deteriorated much more than we had expected. She was grotesquely thin. Her head resembled a skull, her face mottled and discolored with skin like parchment stretched taut across the bones.

In the evening when the family all went into Nana's room to say good night, she asked Chris to kiss her. He hesitated and for that instant we held our collective breath. Then, Chris, remembering his English gentleman father's way of greeting my female friends, lifted her hand and kissed it. We exhaled and were thankful for the natural grace of a child.

Taking risks, at any age, is never easy, but to sidestep the effort is to lack courage and without courage what is our life worth? Often taking risks involves a fight for justice and usually requires perseverance. Is perseverance a first cousin to faith? Can we have faith in God without faith in ourselves? Perhaps this story will help us explore these questions.

My husband, Ernest, is a bloody-minded Englishman. At least that is what he calls himself—I see him as someone with a thirst for justice who will battle on behalf of a good cause for years—even decades, if necessary. His bloody-mindedness is doubly admirable since we live in Canada, the peaceful country. Making waves is not the done-thing here traditionally. He once kept the name of our local library from being changed to a name that neither the library staff nor the community wanted—was part of a group who fought successfully to keep a half-way house for ex-prisoners open by forming the "Stop the Stop, Not In Our Back Yard" movement and when we were first married, through his perseverance and persuasion he provided the inspiration for me to become a non-smoker. He has won other battles, of course, and lost some, but a few years ago he outdid himself.

We decided to take our small-accumulated fortune out of our sock and engage an investment advisor recommended to us by a close acquaintance. We asked the advisor to take over the running of our portfolio that included some long held blue-chip stocks. The advisor said he would rationalize our holdings, whatever that meant. We asked him to invest conservatively and then we sat back to watch our investments grow.

Apparently, our man's definition of conservative differed from ours and when he sold our valuable stocks for "Uncle Willies' corner store" shares and made other highly speculative trades our investments plunged in value.

I was a trifle worried but did my breathing exercises and applied a bit of lotion on the line between my eyebrows.

However, this was but child's play for bloody-minded Ernest.

He began by phoning our investment guy and when his calls were not returned he wrote letters to him—repeatedly. After six months the man finally responded to Ernest's communications with a phone message on his birthday to wish Ernest best regards. Ernest then directed his communications to the employer, one of the largest brokerage firms in North America, headquartered in New York City. After numerous calls and a plethora of letters from Ernest, they replied, "We've done nothing untoward" while our money continued to evaporate like our dreams of a comfortable retirement.

I was now seriously concerned—sleep deprived and developing a tic in my left cheek.

Ernest, however, was undaunted and contacted our local politicians (a feat in itself) who directed him to the Ontario Securities Commission, an organization set up to help in these situations. They suggested he call a lawyer. Of course, we had no money left to pay for lawyers so on he went to the Investment Dealers Association of Canada who granted him an interview and then were never heard from again.

I was becoming catatonic—something like a gerbil on a treadmill under disco lights.

But some kind soul mentioned the then newly established Ombudsman for Banking Services and their representative was almost as parched for justice as Ernest. He looked over the six years and ten pounds of one-way correspondence, agreed that we should feel aggrieved and wrote a compelling report to the brokerage firm who wrote a terse note to us wrapped around a check.

I was relieved. Ernest was exhausted.

We didn't get all our lost money back but we did get a fair percentage of it and Ernest got the satisfaction of knowing that he, a one man office, could get justice from a multimillion dollar corporation.

The press called to interview him. And when they asked, "Mr. Wotton, what is the advice you might give to others in a similar situation?" He replied, "You have to learn to type, stay alive, and be bloody minded."

CHAPTER 5

Fallow Time, Like a Womb, Births Creativity

Scripture Verses: Mark 2:27 and Exodus 23:12

Fallow: "ploughed but left unplanted in order to restore its fertility"

My understanding of fallow time is time that is alive with energy, the kind of energy that a seedling experiences in the rich, prepared earth, that a developing life sustains in the mother's womb, and that a creative idea embodies when it erupts from the recesses of our minds.

I sense an urgency for the creative resources of fallow time in our society today and I often have a strong urge to stop my own busy-ness in order to be nourished and to recover balance, as nature does, on a regular, rhythmic basis.

By definition fallow time is a time of reflection, of letting go of control and shortsighted goals. Fallow time is a vigorous, fertile, and ultimately high-yielding downtime.

It is the reverse side of an action, the yin to accomplishment's yang. It is home to creative imagination. And I believe that creative imagination is the Holy Spirit working through us.

A number of years ago when Ernest and I were consumed with our fledgling careers and Chris was young, we all felt the need for a holiday—at least a few days to stop, relax and have fun—to enjoy laughter and one another's company. Ernest and I both worked from home so we were always at work. We thought it would be good for Christopher to experience another country but in addition to the fact that we couldn't afford to travel, it was February, the middle of the school year and, as always, the middle of work deadlines. It was a particularly rotten February and we were feeling trapped in our apartment. One morning the radio was playing a catchy Jamaican number and when it ended, the program host, who had visited Jamaica, began to laud it as a haven for the weary and playground for all. Christopher said, "Let's go!" First, we all laughed. Then we stopped, thought, and creative imagination kicked in. "Let's have a Jamaican week-end . . . in Toronto."

Christopher, then eight years old said,

"What will we do in Jamaica? Is the food good? Is it hot there? Can I take all my stuff?"

With these questions and others in mind we made a trip to the library for illustrated books of Jamaica, and a visit to the travel agent for brochures. We borrowed some recipes, complete with where to get the ingredients, and some reggae recordings from a Jamaican friend. Ernest rummaged around in the storage room and found a sun lamp saying,

"If we've got to do this we may as well come back with a tan."

Finally, and most important, we covered all our windows with orange, yellow and red tissue paper. We couldn't see the snow and ice outside, but the light came streaming through in brilliant colors. Then we boosted the heat and turned off the phone ready to relax, read and play. We forced ourselves to stop our busyness for just a few days, to have child-like fun and to be refreshingly unproductive. We came "home" as relaxed as unstrung puppets but energized and ready to tackle the rest of winter.

It would be interesting for a church group (or a whole church community) to try this for a day. To choose a theme and transform a space in the church providing "food" for all the senses but no program and then just enter in and be. To do this would take courage and trust in Spirit-filled creative imagination. The group's reflection on their experience a week or two later, in the context of a simple service of prayer, could birth an artistic Sabbath experience. All could come away with an awareness of the life-giving benefits of fallow time.

CHAPTER 6

Community
Our Fertile Land

SCRIPTURE VERSES: ECCLESIASTES 4:9–10 AND JOHN
15:12–15

We all have several communities in our lives. People have a
basic need to gather for companionship, support and hope-
fully deep relationships. Almost all the stories we know
about Jesus took place in community and the Church works
to continue that model.

The heart of any community is communion—the sharing of our lives. The Church's sacrament of Communion is
also the sharing of life, because the sacrament is the people
themselves. This is why I find an invitation to the Communion table that is offered only to the baptized offensive.
It is like inviting guests to dinner but only allowing them
to watch and not eat if you find they haven't subscribed
to your convictions. Jesus welcomed and accepted all. His
model for living was one of caring, inclusive community.

One summer, in search of an inclusive communal experience, Ernest found, in a copy of Engineering Digest, a farmhouse for rent. It was in Sa, a tiny village in northern Portugal just south of Porto. It sounded perfect for our summer holiday. The number to call was in England and the man who answered the phone was a friend of the farmhouse owner. He said, "If you're looking for discos don't come." We immediately booked the house for three weeks in August.

The twelve village farmhouses, of Sa, were crafted of local stone by their owners and were clustered close together, surrounded by the farmlands, mostly vineyards. The terrain was hilly and the views, overlooking the Douro valley, appeared like distant landscape paintings in shades of mauve and green dotted with earth tones.

Our house had modern plumbing and all the kitchen amenities, but it also had the charm of the original stone bread oven and magnificent, oak furniture hand carved by the owner's grandfather. The living quarters were one flight up with a long balcony the length of the house. We knew that half of the ground floor was a wine cellar, as basic a room in northern Portugal as a kitchen is to us, but the other half of the ground floor was a mystery.

As we began to settle in we heard muffled sounds and movement beneath us.

"Did you hear that?" I asked Ernest. "I know wine must breath but I don't think it gets up and moves around."

"Not unless it's in someone's hands," replied Ernest. "The owners will be a hundred miles from here by now; they left to go home over an hour ago."

"They didn't strike me as people who would be holding hostages under the farmhouse" I said. "They were so charming."

"Are you sure? Just because he kissed your hand and doffed his hat to me? They spoke only Portuguese; they could have been saying anything, like I hope they've caught the serial killer who's lose in these parts."

The sounds persisted, so whoever was below us was still alive. Gathering our courage, armed only with lethal umbrellas, we crept down the outside staircase. When we reached the ground we found that the far door was unbolted so we gently opened it and stood back. From the rear of this pitch-dark room seven pairs of eyes attached to seven sheep looked as startled as we felt. We apologized for disturbing them and for maligning their good names.

Later that week we sat on our balcony, sipping wine, and watching Manuel, a spry, wiry haired little man, assisted by his dog Bobby, shear those sheep. Manuel put a sheet of plastic on the ground and laying one animal at a time on the plastic, he tied the back legs and began, with just a pair of scissors, to sheer with amazing speed. Meanwhile Bobby dashed around the plastic on his short terrier legs barking directions to the sheep. At times it was difficult to tell Manuel and Bobby apart. When the shearing was done, Manuel hung the wool over the fence to dry. A few days later a large woman in a flowered, wrap-around skirt seemed to appear from nowhere to fetch the wool to make blankets. Meanwhile, somewhere in Canada, blankets were being woven digitally, untouched by human hands!

The village had narrow stone paths that were both sidewalk and motorway—scaled for the motorbikes that families piled onto. They carried their big, colorful hand-woven baskets as they made their way to the main road and on to the market. The paths were just wide enough to allow the oxen to pull their carts with the enormous wooden wheels down to the fields and back. Sa also possessed the white clapboard chapel that served the surrounding villages. It had battery-powered bells that rang on the quarter hour, twenty-four hours a day. This allowed the men and older children working in the fields to know when it was time for meals but took some getting used to through the night.

This was a true community and we wanted to get to know the people and feel a part of it, but the lack of a common language was keeping us just tourists.

The heart of Sa was the village shop: the one-room ground floor of a house, which sold vegetables from the owner's garden. It had fresh fish and big round loaves of luscious rye bread delivered to it daily, provided the only phone in the village and was the central gathering place for all. On our first day in Sa, we stood looking into the shop bending our 6'8" and 6'2" frames under the doorway and we sensed a crowd gathering behind us. We glanced around and I felt like I was on stage and hadn't learned my lines. But "bom dia" was all that was necessary as they, being small in stature, were just fascinated by our heights. They smiled their welcome to us reminding us that language is more than words.

The young children gathered around the steps of the shop daily to play. The women congregated there to shop and socialize. They gestured an invitation for us to join them and two women introduced us, through mime, to the meal-in-itself rye bread that sustained us thereafter. During our stay a woman's husband died and the grieving, comforting and funeral planning were carried out there. If we were to really get involved with the people of the village it would be on the steps of that shop.

We sometimes strolled to the market town five miles away. On those walks we saw laundry drying on lines along the roadside and sunken tiled "sinks" just off the road in the wooded areas where the women in our village did their laundry. There were empty plastic laundry bottles strewn around and these bottles gave me an idea.

The daughter of the shop family, Rosa—a lovely, slim, outgoing young woman, was in high school and just beginning to learn English. The children would of-ten pull Rosa out of the store to play with them which she did happily. Ernest and I were getting to know the women and children of the village through ever increas-ing mimed "conversations" but we thought, with Rosa's help, we might deepen our new friendships by holding a puppet workshop for the village children.

I invented instant puppets from found objects years ago which I demonstrate at workshops in To-ronto. So for materials we used the discarded laundry bottles, as large sculpted heads, and other found objects such as egg cartons, plastic bags, pieces of string and toilet paper roles as various puppet body parts. There, on the shop steps, the children and we created puppet creatures of all kinds with Rosa as our interpreter and resident artist. One little boy squealed with delight when Rosa announced the project. He chose a large orange detergent bottle for a head with the handle forming a prominent nose. He encouraged the others to embellish their puppets with chicken feathers—which until then the unfortunate chickens were still using.

Rosa led them in a musical performance with their puppets to a Portuguese song they all knew and the audience/community of mothers, chickens, sheep and oxen enjoyed the show enormously. From then on the children carried their creations with them and whenever they saw us, their puppets sang and danced a greeting. Before we left, Rosa made a traditional, multi-colored cloth doll for me which is still featured prominently in our living room.

We attended Eucharist in the little chapel on the Sundays and though the language was Portuguese we could follow along through the familiar rhythm of the liturgy. But our fondest memory and our most moving Communion was with the community on the steps of the village shop.

CHAPTER 7

Humor
Sustenance for Mind and Spirit

SCRIPTURE VERSES: GENESIS 18:11 AND MATTHEW 7:3 & 23:24 AND MARK 4:21 & 10:25 (ALSO SEE NOTE AT END OF CHAPTER)

Humor is often referred to as our saving grace. It can bring us out of conflict and even despair by restoring balance to a situation. The saving moments of humor can be as simple as a look, a wry smile, a gesture or well-placed word or phrase. It can relieve a tense moment. I remember finding myself in a heated and absurd argument at a meeting once. The Chair caught my eye and his look was not one of judgment but bemusement. The look said, do you not see the humor in this situation? And I realized I did and stopped arguing.

Humor is not a structured joke; it is our innate ability to see the ironies and absurdities in life. It also enables us to experience joy and contentment; to save us from taking our day-to-day "crises" and ourselves so seriously. Humor is the characteristic that makes us human.

Actors often complain that a scene is too dark or dramatic to contain humor, but to be true to life every scene does contain humor so the actor or storyteller must find it.

It would be unnatural not to recall humorous stories from the life of a loved one at his/her funeral—humor provides strength and healing for the mind and spirit in the way that food and rest do for the body.

In fact, physiologically (by ancient definition), humor is our fluid or juice—our very essence.

And what better time to exercise our sense of humor than when producing the annual Christmas Pageant!

Whatever your faith background, and North America has them all, December seems to be the time of year to tell the traditional stories. In my case it was all about Christmas Pageants. Not so long ago I directed not one but a number of these Pageants for my sins. My theatre background convinced several different churches each year that I was the one to keep the story, the nostalgia and the warm feeling of Christmas alive in their communities. The trouble was that, like everyone else, I had tons of shopping, and entertaining, and decorating and what passes for baking and, if there was time, the rest of my work to do. I should be at the mall! And added to that the first pageant was in early December when we are still raking the leaves and putting the garden tools away.

So each fall I was overwhelmed by the prospect of finding sixty adult volunteer actors and four or five sets of parents with infants who are up for performing out of doors on a December evening. It turned out they actually enjoyed it! The show was presented on eight stages along a path in the churchyard. Audiences were guided past the scenes—a new audience every five minutes for four hours—four hours! A light fall of snow was always welcome but we did all the anti-rain dances we knew.

One year for this pageant there were two choirs, five holy families with six infants (one set of twins), three life sized puppets and sixty-two actors, no animals—perhaps another year. The show was double cast so that all could take turns getting warm in-doors. Of course, the performers arrive on the day wearing multiple coats, long johns and thick wool socks. No problem—the medieval costumes, made from twenty-seven pairs of discarded drapes, are large enough to cover any size parka. A few came wearing your basic biblical Adidas,

"But these are the only shoes I have" they say, hoping white canvas shoes sticking out at the bottom of an ornate period costume with velvet folds, gilt trim and feathered turban won't be noticed. Sandals and extra socks are found. Mind you, some have no wardrobe limitations. When the last Mary and Joseph came in from the Bethlehem scene Mary removed her costume to reveal a full-length mink coat. Apparently, carpentry is the trade to be in.

The holy families became a little extended family group between performances sharing baby stories and baby equipment. One infant had an enviable, thick head of black hair and Silent Night put him to sleep. A woman in the audience said,

"Look it's a doll, what a shame they couldn't get a real baby"—which caused the mother to blurt out,

"No, look again, this is a real baby!"

I'm sure the original Mary would have done the same.

Then before I could finish my cast party pizza I was on to the next—an indoor production. This one is done with very small children—guaranteed to get oohs, ahhs and chuckles from the adults. They were doing just fine until the sheep fight broke out at the high altar. For all but the sheep's parents it was the high light of the production.

Still recovering from tiny tantrums and backstage mothers I was thrown into the pageant that used live animals. The organizers got them from a petting zoo the day before the event. The "little" lamb we were expecting, for a shepherd to carry under his arm, weighed 200 pounds. There were no donkeys so we made do with a llama who required exercise. She was walked around the block before the service on Christmas morning. There are now several people who live in the neighborhood of that church who have sworn off drinking on Christmas Eve.

Tearing myself away from the menagerie, I embarked on pageant number four. This was done with teenagers who devised a modern version of the Christmas story. The characters were Joseph, a downsized office worker, Mary, an undiscovered artist, the Angel, who enters the scene through Mary's painting—a tricky little stunt using cloth on a frame, a back light and plenty of Velcro—and a slum landlord who finds room for the Holy Family in his leaky basement. The younger children played rodents (think urban sheep). Oh and the shepherds were grandparents in a senior citizens' home.

"I think the shepherds should be grandparents" said Katherine aged 11, "They comfort and care for everybody but they're made to feel separate from the rest of us."

The actor's lines were improvised throughout—an old story told anew.

I've come to think that directing this traditional story in December (even several times) really beats hanging out at the mall. However, when December moves into gear and people ask me if I'm ready for Christmas I find it hard to believe it hasn't already happened.

And another "nativity story"—this one is of four legged family members who also bring humor and joy to our lives.

It was raining cats and dogs—well actually just cats. Four tiny ginger kittens were huddled under a pile of wood next to the fence in our back garden and it was teeming with rain. Chris, then 13, had spotted them earlier in the day so when the rains came he and Ernest gathered them up and brought them inside. When I came home there they were, a warm furry heap, in a box in the corner of the kitchen.

It was September and we had got to know this furry heap's mother over the summer. She was obviously homeless and pregnant. Ours was a caring neighborhood so she got better fed as her pregnancy became more obvious. She came to the door and uttered a kind of cat's version of you hoo but refused to come inside, preferring take-out meals on the doorstep.

The kittens chose early August to be born but not under the woodpile next to the fence. Apparently, mother cats move their litters from place to place for safety and we first saw the family in their mum's chosen birthplace on a shelf in the back of the garage—the kittens nestled in a box of three-inch nails!

I remembered feeling like I was in just such a place when I gave birth.

We lived in the upper half of a duplex and often left the front door at the bottom of the stairs open during the warm weather. As I gazed at these four little month old refugees I heard "Mum's" plaintive call at the door. For the first time she accepted the invitation to come in and followed me to the cardboard box in the kitchen. She took a good look inside the box and then turned and walked back through the apartment, down the stairs and out. We didn't have her down as an abandoner so the three of us went to the window in the back bedroom, which over looked the garden, and waited. Sure enough she came around and headed for the woodpile to see if her lot were still there. Having satisfied herself that somehow her kittens had found their way into our kitchen she returned, marching straight to the cardboard box—her new home. In less than half an hour we went from a family without pets to one with five cats.

We did a little research and found it would be ten weeks minimum before they were weaned. Mum soon got them out of the box and moving around and then the most frequently uttered phrase in our home was, "Don't step on the cat!"

As the kittens had been born and had lived in the "wild" for a month their Mum had taught them to keep out of sight, especially while napping. They began to find obscure hiding places between feedings and group play times. They came out at the sound of Mum's special dinnertime call from such places as the back of the fridge, behind sofa and chairs and from the loft of a Fisher Price barn, which was itself in the back of a closet. Neighbor children came over to see the kittens and often we just couldn't find them. But when the family was on view it was fascinating to watch not just the kittens but also Mum's parenting techniques. When the kittens played, Mum tipped over a wicker wastebasket and crawled into it where she could discretely watch over them through the wicker latticework. There was one kitten not as strong as the others and she would take him to an out of the way spot and feed him and talk to him.

The weeks soon passed and we reluctantly faced the fact that five cats would be more than we or the apartment could cope with. We thought Mum and one kitten, we had named Min, would make a nice addition to our family so we prepared a flyer advertising the others as "New Fall Furs no money down until 3006." We didn't have to distribute this flyer however, because we announced their availability, with photos and the harrowing tale of their birth, at our son's school—it was a piece of cake or deluxe cat chow. We could have found homes for a dozen adorable kittens.

Mum and Min made a move across town with us, when we bought a house, and Min had a litter of her own—another story. They were good company keeping us amused and mouse free for many years. They have both died of old age now and though we have less vacuuming to do, no vet bills and no torn window screens, there is something missing. Unfortunately, it's not mice, so if there is a homeless cat reading this, we are accepting photos and resumes.

Note: Both the Old Testament and the New Testament are full of humor. When the Old Testament stories were first told much of the humor was in the larger-than-life telling; something like street theatre. Reread Proverbs and imagine the stories being acted out. And Jesus was a master at one-liners and humorous images. Reread the parables and Jesus's conversations with the Pharoses.

CHAPTER 8

Hope, Like Prayer, Makes All Things Well

Scripture Verses: Job 14:7–9 and Romans 8:24

Hope has the power to reframe our thoughts, give us confidence to act or allay our deepest fears.

Hope in action is prayer.

I was flat on my back on a hospital gurney and kept my eyes tightly closed. I had the sense I was in a large crowded room with many others who also needed help and perspiration was soaking through my blouse in the August heat. In my self-imposed darkness I felt threatened by the noise and jostling movement around me. I called out, frequently, "Does anyone speak English?" Apparently no one did. When the heavy swinging door opened I swear I heard a pig squealing.

Ernest and I had taken a taxi and then a train from the tiny Portuguese village of Sa, where we had been enjoying our holiday, to Lisbon as soon as I recognized the symptoms.

Once inside the hospital we spotted an empty gurney and I laid down on it with eyes firmly shut. Ernest slowly eased the gurney into a large waiting area before going to find a phone to change our flight. I held the belief that the procedure when your retina was detaching was to lie down—eyes closed—get medical help. I knew what was happening to me because this wasn't my first experience. The first detachment, ten years before, led to two failed operations and total blindness in my right eye—not the best part of my fortieth birthday celebration. But that time I was home in Toronto with friends standing by to help, excellent medical facilities and one good eye to guide me. I was surprisingly calm that first time—I thought there are many things I value dearly that I only have one of—my heart, my husband, my child. I felt all would be well. This time, far away from home, I knew the signs but not the language and I had no spare eye—all did not seem so well.

Finally, my hopes, prayers and verbal pleas were answered. Kind hands appeared and wheeled me out of the large space into a small, quiet room.

"You may sit up and open your eyes, you know," a strange voice said.

I reluctantly did as I was directed and saw a small man with dark hair and warm brown eyes in a white coat.

"But," I said, "my retina is detaching,"

"We no longer lie down in darkness with a retina detachment", he assured me. "We get to the operating room as fast as possible."

My retina was detaching slowly this time and it was like looking over the top of a lacy, black mountain. It was painless but the fear of slipping back down that mountain into total darkness made me tense from head to toes. The doctor peered into my eye and concurred with my diagnosis.

From what I could see the rooms and old fashioned iron framed beds appeared clean and tidy and there was a reassuring medicinal smell but the space looked sparsely equipped—rather like the simple homes in Sa. I asked the key question,

"Should I have the operation here, now?"

He answered, "If it were I, I would go home to Canada."

Part of me felt relieved, clearly neither the doctor nor I thought this was the best place to have an operation, especially with my unsuccessful history. My hope began to flag as fear threatened to take over. Would we be able to get an immediate flight home in August? Was my surgeon available—might he be on holiday? Was Ernest able to contact anyone? And, all the time, I was slowly slipping down the mountain.

Meanwhile Ernest through prayer and perseverance managed to change our airline reservations and struggle through a call to Canada, with a Portuguese-only speaking operator, to talk with a friend who would contact my surgeon.

When we arrived in Toronto we went straight to the hospital where I had the operation the next day under local anesthetic and tranquilizers. Being awake during your eye operation is a story in itself:

Dr. to nurse, "I need a number 47 needle."

Nurse to Dr., "I don't see one, I'm looking but I. . . don't find one."

"Have you looked over there?"

"Yes, but no 47—will a 59 do?"

"No, it has to be a 47."

And a distant salesman's voice in the corner of the room was giving the details of a new product to my surgeon and I was aware of a student next to me learning all about reattaching a retina. But I was so relaxed that my thoughts and concerns were in slow motion and seemed almost impersonal.

"Oooh, I do hope you find the #47—have you looked everywhere? Nooo, don't bother him with that product now, it's not one I need; let him read about it later." And, ". . . goodness, go back to the classroom—stop distracting him with your questions."

The information filtered through my drugged brain—more like a scene from Frankenstein than a lived experience.

That was several years ago and my one eye still sees me through work and play.

I value my sight as much as anyone—we live in a visual society and it's impossible to imagine not being able to see. But when I remember my experience in Portugal I don't immediately think of my eye—I recall the beauty of the countryside, the taste of that rye bread and the joy of the children with their puppets. I think of our friends who met us at the airport with an ambulance who simply said, "It's wonderful to be given the opportunity to help" and, of course, I think of Ernest who through heat, stress and the Portuguese language pressed on with what had to be done. If I do eventually lose the rest of my sight I will still have the pictures in my head of my life experiences, "good" and "bad" and the stories that go with them. And somehow, with hope, all will be well.

CHAPTER 9

Of the Earth,
Not On the Earth

Scripture Verses: Job 12:7–10 and Psalm 148: 1–10 and, of course, Paul's first letter to the Corinthians 12: 12–26 mentioned below

Our sacred stories reflect our passions and these stories become our new New Testament. Regard for the Earth is one passion I have long held; I express it here in a garden-variety rant.

I am a snob. I don't consider a cramped space surrounded by noxious fumes, rolling along a river of pot holes a luxury. I resent parting with my life savings in order to park, license, fuel and insure my transportation. I eschew those folk wrapped in their second skin of glimmering steel. In short the mere mention of the automobile, whether magnificent Mercedes or second hand Cessna, is my cue to depart—on foot.

Being in-car-cerated robs me of the experience of weather, the intimacy of my environment and regular casual encounters with neighbors—two legged and four legged. It encourages isolation and a belief that getting there is more important than the journey. When time is a factor I ride my bicycle, enjoying the breeze and the heady sense of freedom—the closest a mortal comes to flying. If the distance to my destination is great I take the subway. For grocery shopping there is the convenience of delivery, just shop and walk away, and when there's too much snow and ice I call a taxi. They know me by name.

All in all I have a chosen, preferred life style that does not include owning an automobile. It began many years ago out of concern for the environment but has become, quite simply, a more pleasant and comfortable way to travel. As side benefits, not owning a car promotes a healthier, active lifestyle and probably saves me thousands of dollars a year.

Sooo, when people offer to pick me up in their car for some social occasion or to give me a lift home after a meeting, when they live nowhere near me, I despair.

I've tried to explain that I have transport of a different kind and have no need of a ride but it's,

"No, no, no we won't hear of it. In you go, here let me move those papers and things, hope you're not too cramped with your long legs, don't mind the pop bottles—Trixie down! Get into the back seat, the nice lady is going to ride with us."

I am faced with the dilemma of thanking them for including me in their beloved rolling homestead or I can say, "No thank you, I choose to be transported in comfort." I often do the latter. I have fewer friends than most people.

Don't get me wrong if a person is a neighbor or even lives in the same part of town I'm delighted to ride with that person either in his/her car or my taxi or we could both cycle. It's the one-car one-driver syndrome and the utter dependency on that car that drives me to rant—the assumption that if you are not traveling in a privately owned automobile you are deprived, extravagant or mad.

I do realize that some people's professions require the use of a car especially when public transit is limited. However, it seems to me that many people just have not considered the classier non-car way.

Picture a city where the sidewalks are well lit for pedestrians, instead of lit by the spill from streetlights designed for cars. Imagine secure bicycle paths on main thoroughfares with well-placed guard blocks that cars and trucks couldn't cross and envisage four-wheeled traffic in the city core limited to taxis, streetcars, buses, delivery and emergency vehicles. Heaven!

Of course, there are models of improved transport all over the world—car pooling, car-free days, minimum passenger lanes and fuel cell cars, come to mind. Statistics Canada tells us there are more than a billion bicycles in the world and electric car sales are increasing in Canada. Though these cars will not exercise our bodies or connect us to our neighbors they will improve the environment so there's a glimmer of hope.

But while we wait in hope for others to fall out of love with the automobile we snobs will continue to meet each other on the sidewalks, cycle paths and subways.

And to continue our thoughts of the environment on a more poetic level, I share the beliefs of one of my favorite theologians.

Thomas Berry, renowned priest, theologian and ecologist urged us, throughout his lifetime, to recognize humanity and all living beings as of the Earth not on the earth—that all life is subject; not object. Only when we fully grasp these truths might we be able to regard our body, the earth, to be as precious as our own individual bodies.

Perhaps such deep understanding begins with stories. If God is working in us and through us, and I believe God is, it seems to me that we are obliged to blend our own sacred stories with those that have come before ours keeping the Gospel living and growing.

I have taken the liberty of rewriting the Apostle Paul's beautiful letter to the Corinthians to give it a slightly different interpretation.

An ecological version of St. Paul's First letter to the Corinthians 12: 12–26

For just as the earth is one and has many members, and all the members of the earth, though many, are one body, so it is with Christ. For in the one Spirit we were all baptized in the one body—sun, water or air—soil, plants or creatures and we were all made to drink of one Spirit. Indeed, the earth does not consist of one member but of many. If the rock would say, "Because I am not a frog I do not belong to the earth" that would not make her any less a part of the earth. And if the man would say, "Because I am not vegetation I do not belong to the earth" that would not make him any less a part of the earth. And if the lake said, "Because I am not the sun's rays I am not a part of the earth" that would not make her any less a part of the earth. If the whole earth were a lake where would we stand? If the whole earth were soil how would we drink? But as it is, God arranged the members of the earth, each one of them, as he chose. If all were a single member, where would the earth be? As it is there are many members, yet one earth. The person cannot say to the polar bear, "I have no need of you" nor again the tree to the bird, "I have no need of you." On the contrary, the members of the earth that seem to be weaker are indispensable, and those members of the earth that we think less honorable we clothe with greater honor, and our less respectable members are treated with greater respect whereas our more respectable members do not need this. But God has so arranged the earth, giving the greater honor to the inferior member, that there may be no dissension within the earth but the members may have the same care for one another. If one member suffers, all suffer together with him, if one member is honored, all rejoice together with her.

And I offer this prayer for all living beings of the earth:

Be still and know Creation aches
Be still and know Creation mourns
Be still and know Creation . . . heals

Be still and know Creation
Be still and know
Be still

Illustration 1:

Illustration 2a:

Illustration 2b:

Illustration 2c:

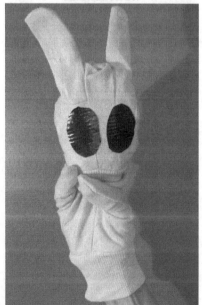

Illustration 2b:

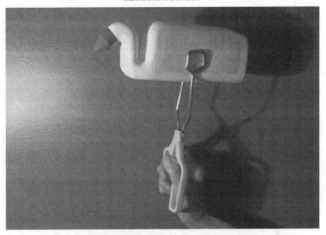

Illustration 3:

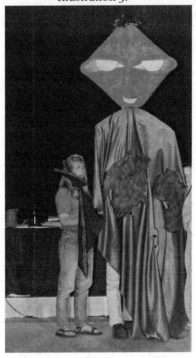

Illustration 4:

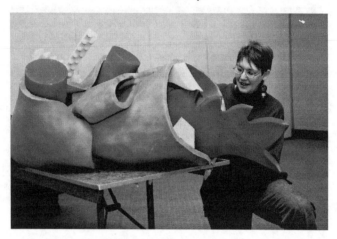

PART 2

An Actor's Tools for Life and Liturgy

CHAPTER 1

The Body
An Actor's Instrument of Movement

Just as the violinist's instrument is the violin and the painter's instruments are brush and canvas, the actor's instruments are the body and voice. And all arts require a honing of the creative imagination. Therefore to make use of the craft of acting one must develop and then care for these instruments.

Acting mirrors life at its largest and so the skills for acting are also the skills for living.

The body needs daily exercise to perform at its best—we hear this from everyone concerned with the health and wellbeing of the human body. So it is as essential to walk, swim, ski, row or do whatever exercise that is enjoyable to you, the performer, regularly as it is for the pianist to run through scales and chosen pieces of music regularly.

And before rigorous exercise, including rehearsals, comes the warm-up—the gentle exercise that reintroduces the body to itself and reminds us, each day, that our bodies, minds, and spirits are one. When working with a group it is especially important to begin a learning session or rehearsal with warm-ups. This involves stretching for the body followed by a simple theatre game (described in chapter four) to awaken our creativity, make eye contact with others, and literally be in touch.

We move on three basic planes—up, down, and from side to side. It is useful to have an appreciation of this in order to know which plane we are most at home in and which we may be neglecting. Moving only on one plane is monotonous for the viewer and may make us appear (and become) stiff. Allowing the body to use a variety of planes lends drama and life to a scene.

YOUR PLANE

In a standing position close your eyes and without thinking about it extend one arm out in front of you. Hold your arm there and open your eyes. A high mover's arm and torso will be slanted upward above chest level. A useful level for liturgical drama as churches usually have high, high ceilings and we tend not to regard this upper space. A center or level plane mover will find her arm extended directly out from her chest. This, by far, is the most commonly used plane in our standing and chair-sitting society. And the low mover will be pointing downward, the rarest automatic space used except perhaps by dancers.

STRETCHES

If in a group, form a circle to feel connected while leaving ample space between you for movement.

Stand erect (with knees slightly flexed, never locked, to protect the back) with chest high and shoulders relaxed—feet apart approximately the width of your shoulders, toes pointing straight ahead. Raise your arms in a big stretch which will cause you to yawn—enjoy this. If you are in a group, you are all sharing the same air and water vapor literally becoming one.

Then, extend your right arm up and out to the right, attempt to touch the ceiling, turning eyes, body, and focus toward your outstretched finger tips. Always remember to keep breathing—stretch from the belly. To test your full stretch try moving just from the shoulder then from the middle of you and notice the inches of increase in the stretch. Repeat this exercise to the left. The body always cries out for balance.

Next cross your arms over your chest as though pulling off a sweater—continue in a fluid circular arc. Bend your knees as much or little as is comfortable for you, gathering the shared breath and pouring it down over you from the top of your head. In so doing you are con spiring with creation. Repeat this exercise two or three times.

To loosen and stretch the hips (very important as most of us spend so much time operating from the center plane—sitting or standing) bend the knees and place your hands on your legs just above the knee and stick your bum out. Hold your knees as still as possible and rotate your hips in a circle for 10 rotations and then reverse direction and rotate another 10 times. If in a group this is another reason for standing in a circle as no one can see this exercise from behind!

Finally, return to the erect position described above and imagine a thread attached to the center of your raised chest (shoulders relaxed) running up to a track on the ceiling. Imagine being pulled by that thread, chest leading, around the room with feet rolling from heal to toes. Keep breathing. You should feel light and fluid as you move.

This is a six-minute exercise routine to start your day, class or rehearsal relaxed and comfortable with your body and with others.

The body also needs to experience full relaxation routinely to combat stress, tension, and fatigue. I have found that teenagers, in particular, appreciate the following exercise.

RELAXATION

Lie down on your back, arms at your sides, and ankles uncrossed on the floor or on your bed. If on the floor, place a small rolled up towel behind your neck. Remove shoes, watches, and ties, anything that is restrictive and make sure you are comfortable. Begin with deep breathing and continue this breathing throughout the exercise. Clench the toes on your left foot as tightly as you can, hold for 3 seconds and release—do not hold your breath! Continue this clench and release with each body part working your way up your left side to the top of your head and then down your right side ending with the toes on your right foot. Focus your mind on each body part with each clench and release and continue breathing. Include ankle, calf, thigh, buttocks, side of torso, upper arm, lower arm, fingers into a fist, shoulder, neck, scalp, and face. During this exercise note specifically where your body holds tension. With this information, you can clench and release the tension in that part of you when the need arises. Complete the exercise by tensing your entire body and releasing. Get up slowly and carefully, rolling onto one side and use your arms to push yourself to a sitting position first. If you have been breathing deeply, more oxygen may have gone to your head than usual. Allow your lightheadedness to clear before standing.

A word about the body on stage:

It is helpful to know stage directions for reading plays and directing actors. Up stage is the back of the stage or chancel and down stage is nearest the audience. This is because in Shakespeare's time stages were raked (slanted downward from back to front) for visibility. Stage right and stage left are the actor's right and left when facing the audience. Center stage is, of course, center. So it is easy to determine up left, down right down center etc. and the wall that isn't there, the space between players and audience, we call the fourth wall. When there is an arbitrary choice, play to the fourth wall for visibility and intimacy.

The game Stage Picture (described in Chapter Three) is a means of assisting players to find interesting and re-laxed positions. A player's back can be toward the audience as long as the player is not delivering a long speech and remember it is always the player's responsibility not to be-come visually blocked. It is never the responsibility of the player who is blocking another to move. If you look straight ahead and cannot see some of the audience that means they can't see you either so discretely move.

CHAPTER 2

The Voice

An Actor's Instrument of Sound

Voice is largely dependent on correct breathing. Unfortunately, we start to develop poor breathing habits early in childhood and so we need to relearn to breathe the way we did as infants. Deep breathing down to our diaphragms is the key not only to producing strong voice but also for good health. Our bodies need the regular cleansing of breath moving in and out of the center of us to remove impurities and tensions. Regularly inhaling down to the diaphragm is the only way to produce and maintain a strong voice. The diaphragm is a muscle that runs right across our middle just below the rib cage. It is cone shaped when at rest. When our intake of breath is deep enough it will flatten the cone and when we speak on the exhale (we can't speak on an inhale) the cone will bounce up and propel our voice up and out. No other muscles are needed for the production of voice. Our voices are potentially the last part of us to wear out but so many elderly people have thin, faint, creaky

voices that show a lifetime of shallow breathing. When we
allow our intake of breath to stop in the middle of our chest
or at the base of our throat we have to use other muscles to
produce voice in addition to the tasks they are intended to
do so that over time these muscles wear out. Well trained
actors can maintain strong resonate voices well into their
eighties and even nineties.

Shallow breathing becomes a habit usually precipitated
by tension; even very slight tension will cause us to quicken
our breath. Deep breathing will relax us but we need to be
conscious of our breathing to break our poor habits and
get ourselves on a healthier, strong voice-producing course.
Some people have been breathing shallowly for so long they
can no longer recall what correct breathing feels like. Here
is an exercise to test your breathing:

Lie on the floor (if this is impossible, sprawl on a chair),
place a large, heavy book on your abdomen, and breathe.
Try to visualize your breath coming in through your nose,
and going straight down a channel in your chest to your diaphragm. If the book moves your breathing is deep enough,
if not, try again. Once you achieve deep breathing repeat
the exercise until you are completely familiar with how it
feels to breathe deeply. You can then "turn on" deep breath
when you feel slight tension and want to be relaxed or when
you need to lift the volume of your voice. This may sound
easier than it is. Relearning to breathe really correctly can
often take years. Breaking old habits and reinstituting new
ones takes perseverance.

To be heard at a distance requires both breath and
energy. If you apply energy to your voice while breathing
shallowly, the sound becomes a shout or even a scream
which will damage your vocal chords. To test your vocal
energy control, go into a church worship space or other
large room. Ideally, ask some others to sit in the middle of

the room and at the back of the room to give you feed back on the following three different levels of energy:

Speak improvisationally for 2 minutes or so to an imaginary person right next to you at a conversational level. Note how that feels.

Lift your energy and speak as above to the middle of the room. Picture your breath going down to your dia-phragm. Now imagine your energy lying just below your breath pushing up and out as you speak. Note the difference of energy needed for this compared to conversation.

Dial up your energy still higher and speak as before to the back of the room. Again, note the difference in how this feels. If you allow yourself to first feel your breath go down to the diaphragm before applying vocal energy you will not shout or scream but you will be heard comfortably.

For those who want to make a thorough study of breath and voice I recommend the book *Freeing the Natural Voice* by Kristen Linkleter.

ENUNCIATION

Now that you have relearned to breath and have control over your vocal energy levels, your words have to be un-derstood! Here is an exercise to do regularly for muscle strengthening in the jaw, tongue and lips and for relieving tension in that area before public speaking.

Stretch your lips and jaw as hard and far as you can from side to side and up and down, stick your tongue out as far as you can in all four directions (try to touch your nose). Your mother was wrong; your face won't freeze that way. I like to imagine the reaction of the congregation if you do this in the pulpit before your sermon.

Now test to see that you have relaxed your jaw by ex-haling with energy through relaxed but un-parted lips. If the sound you produce is that of a horse exhaling, you have succeeded but if the result is smooth air, repeat the exercise until you can make the vibrating, horse-like sound. Doing this exercise regularly will strengthen the muscles needed for enunciation and allow you to control your speech. In the short term it relaxes those muscles giving you more flexibility in speech.

To perform daily exercises with thought and care—to relearn to breathe deeply and to set aside regular time to care for our bodies are some of the many ways we can prolong the life of our actor's instruments for movement and sound.

CHAPTER 3

Our Leadership Style Tells a Story

I'm a strong supporter of a learner as teacher and teacher as learner approach to education. I do believe that we are all, children and adults, teachers and learners at the same time throughout our lives.

So often if we are in a teaching role, we are afraid to show or do what is natural and honest—to expose our vulnerabilities because we think we are expected to know all the answers. This not only interferes with our own opportunity to learn from a situation and from others but it makes us less approachable so that others find it harder to learn from us. This uneven state of affairs, which I call the guru style of teaching, is reflected in our design of space as well as our words and mannerisms. A typical classroom or lecture hall still has a desk or podium in the front with chairs lined up facing it. A typical church has a raised chancel with pews or chairs lined up facing it. The assumption being that the knowledge will be poured down from the front of the space by the leaders to the masses, not shared with all by all.

Flexible space gives greater opportunity for flexibility generally with no upper and lower levels. Sitting in a circle or arc allows us to see one another and tell our stories fully with our bodies as well as our voices

The arrangement of furniture and space also has theological implications. Where do we find God—above and beyond us only, or also in our midst and in one another?

Even when we are arranged in a circle we can slip into a less equal style of leadership. The practice of going around the circle for input on a question, if it is anything more threatening than our names, makes some people uncomfortable as it doesn't permit individuals to respond at their own pace.

Our tendency as teachers to ask questions to which we know the "correct" answer is very much in the guru style. This leaves students looking for the answers they think we want to hear rather than teacher and learner exploring a question together. Once there was a minister telling a story to a group of children who were obviously conditioned to guru leadership. The minister wanted the children to participate and so he described something that he wanted them to name, "It is about so big, is furry, has a bushy tail, and loves to eat nuts—come on, you know what this is—anyone?" A little girl timidly raised her hand and said, "I know the answer is Jesus, but it really sounds like a squirrel."

Narrative theology is not compatible with the guru style. It does not tell us how to think nor does it imply right or wrong answers or interpretations. For narrative theology to be effective the homilist needs to find or create a story that for the homilist reflects the theme or Gospel for that occasion. Then simply tell the story, allowing the listeners to make the connections.

As to presentation, I maintain that telling the stories, both the Scripture stories and the homilist's story of reflection is far more effective than reading them. When material is read the book or papers create a barrier between teller and listener breaking a connecting thread between them. I include memorization tips later in this book, as I know that learning a story for telling is more work than simply reading it. I'm convinced, however, that actually telling the stories will go a long way toward revitalizing the Church by returning us to our narrative roots and creating a sense of intimacy. This takes time but I think the sharers of Scripture could be at least as well prepared as many choirs are with their mid-week practice and before service warm-ups. And providing an opportunity for discussion of the story after the service gives everyone, homilist included, the chance to gain new insights.

Two final words about leadership—if you are fortunate enough to have others working with you to create a liturgy, have at least one meeting with everyone on the team together for planning. Sharing the details of the stories, prayers, music, "choreography," etc. will result in a smooth liturgical experience that flows and brings the congregation fully into the worship.

And remember that audience members at a dramatic production or lecture/presentation/sermon also have an active leadership role. Any actor will tell you that a play has good and not so good performances even though the same actors say the same words in basically the same way on the same stage. The differences, of course, come from the audience response. This is true in any public performance including a liturgy. Our job as audience, and we are all in the "house" or the nave at some time, is to provide the energy from the fourth wall. Our reactions to what is being presented feed the performers or leaders. If they perceive little or no response it is difficult for them to keep their own energy up. When something amuses you, as an audience member don't just smile; make yourself laugh out loud. And just as the speaker is remembering to smile at the audience/congregation you need to smile back. Many of us have a set scowl on our faces when we are concentrating or listening intently—try to break that habit. But, of course, when serious or dramatic material is presented to us there is no greater gift from audience to player than complete silence. Good audience skills improve any performance greatly and everyone benefits.

When giving feedback to all participants in leadership, give positive feedback first then constructive criticism. Both are needed but there is always something good about a presentation so the positive must be genuine and it must be first because creative people see beauty first.

CHAPTER 4

Acting Essentials through Improvisation and Theatre Games

This chapter is aimed at facilitators/directors of groups who are learning skills together or preparing to perform together. However, individuals can also benefit from much of this chapter. There are many books on theatre games for teaching theatre skills but I will describe a few of the games that I use in my teaching.

One of the beauties of learning or rehearsing through games is that the skill is learned in a group. If the group is rehearsing for a liturgical drama and someone is having a problem (too wooden, bad pacing, etc.) you can stop rehearsal and play the appropriate game without pointing out an individual's weakness. This may solve the problem and everyone will benefit. It is a good idea to teach a series of games before the start of a rehearsal schedule so that they can be called upon easily. Tell the group what acting skill the game teaches as you introduce it.

Theatre games are a style of improvisation (improv), and improv has four rules. As acting mirrors life, writ large, these rules serve us well in life as well as in performance.

RULES OF IMPROVISATION/THEATRE GAMES

Rule One: The audience, half of class not presently playing, tells the players who they are i.e., doctors, children, animal trainers (not usually specific characters or people but a group identity) and where they are, always naming a place one would not expect to find the who. Sometimes the audience tells the players the what, an activity the who are doing when the game begins. With the audience giving this information the players have no opportunity to plan, which is the essence of improvisation and the essence of real conversation. Giving unexpected wheres and whats to the whos (baseball players in a shopping mall knitting) provides a creative jumping off point for the players.

Rule Two: The players must try to use and trust their first thoughts. This is difficult for most of us to do because we spend our lives being trained and training ourselves to edit what we say and do. However, the pacing of the scene and its general success, and consequent positive feedback to the players is dependent on trusting one's first thoughts.

Rule Three: No creative blocking of self or others. If a player has established a fictional fact, this cannot be negated by another player because the scene will come to a halt in confusion. For instance, if a player enters, saying to another player, "Mommy, mommy I'm home" that first player has established the identity of both characters. So if the second player says, "Who are you? I don't have any children" that is creative blocking because she has negated the fictional fact that the first player has established. Such a denial may get a laugh but at the expense of the scene. This also applies to the where and the what. The Players, as characters, can dislike or even hate the established fictional facts but they must accept them as facts. Students soon become aware of creative blocking when it occurs both in performance and in life.

Rule Four: Accept the Offer. If a player offers an idea in a scene the other player(s) need to accept that offer or idea and build on it rather than refusing it or avoiding it. For instance, if a player enters with an imaginary tray of cookies saying, "I've brought you this tray of cookies" and the other player responds, "I've just eaten; set them down over there" s/he is not engaging in creative blocking but has not accepted the offer. The second player could have said, "Oh they're my favorite let's get the dill pickles and have a picnic" or "Great they'll be perfect to plaster the holes in that wall." The scene/game will be lively and satisfying only if all players work together and build on one another's offers.

I always begin with a warm-up game; this is a nonthreatening game that gets everyone working together immediately but does not put anyone on the spot. Theatre games teach skills and they are often like mini performances. This book shares professional acting techniques but is not aimed at professional actors so if a high-performance game is introduced before the group members are comfortable with one another the game can be quite painful for some.

One warm-up game which also teaches pacing is Imaginary Ball.

IMAGINARY BALL

The group forms a circle and the designated leader holds an imaginary ball. The size and weight of the ball is obvious by the way it is held. Throw the ball to someone in the circle who must try to catch it exactly when it arrives. That person throws it to someone else and on it goes. From time to time the leader can call out "change" and the one holding the ball at that moment then throws another type of ball. Eventually most will be able to catch the ball on time. You can also use this game for name learning by calling out your name when you catch the ball or calling out the name of the person to whom it is thrown.

Another warm up game is Object in the Circle. This teaches spontaneity, creativity and the fact that acting is showing not telling.

OBJECT IN THE CIRCLE

Players form a circle with an object, chosen at random, in the center. (The object should be non-breakable and large enough to be easily seen) A player steps forward and uses the object as something that its shape suggests to him/her and the others guess what it is. The identity of the object can be anything except what it actually is. The player can also speak but cannot name the object. The players step forward as the Spirit moves them, as often as they like or not at all.

One game I always use when teaching liturgical drama is Stage Picture. It teaches how to be visible and visually interesting as a group and it teaches creative imagination and give and take in a scene.

STAGE PICTURE

Have 3 to 6 people gather in front of the rest of the group. Ask them to move around each other in the designated performance space, making eye contact as they pass one another. Keep breathing from the diaphragm and keep moving until the facilitator calls out "stage picture." The players then strike a pose that is interesting but not uncomfortable as they will have to hold it while the "audience" gives them their who, what and where. Remind the players that they have arms and that they can use any of the three planes but if they are going to sit or lie down on the floor or if they are shorter than the others they will need to be in the front or down stage for visibility. Remember the basic rule—if you can't see a portion of the audience then they can't see you—therefore, move yourself discretely into view.

Then the "audience" will tell them:

What they were reacting to when they froze into this stage picture? For example, if most are looking up maybe a meteor is falling from the sky, or if some look frightened perhaps an escaped lion is coming toward them.

Who they are—either as a group (easiest) or as individuals.

Where they are (remember that the who, what and where should be illogical giving the players a creative jump start)

Then let the scene begin with players speaking and acting using the above information. The facilitator can call an end but as the players become more experienced they will sense an appropriate ending. Finally, do it again with audience as players and players as audience.

For resources on theatre games see Further Reading at the back of this book.

CHAPTER 5

Developing a Character

When actors begin to develop a character they look for any information known about that character first. Working with a script or story, biblical or other literature the actor notes the actions of her character and everything that is said about her character by other characters in the text. Then the actor has a given premise on which to add imaginative detail and description to the character's biography and personality. You may, of course, move your known characters into a different time period or setting from their original ones. This devise can often point out the timelessness of the character and story. Obviously, if you are creating an original character there are no limitations to your imagination.

In creating a character make decisions regarding physical appearance, age, likes, dislikes, personality traits—the background and history of the character's actions, family, friends, work, and the significant events of her/his life. Out of that information, experiment with how the character will walk and move.

Then find your character's voice. It is wise to avoid national or regional accents unless you are extremely familiar with the particular accent, as it will need to be authentic and consistent. Experiment with how the personality of your character would speak—hesitant, timid, brash, confident, educated, etc.

For both movement and voice observe and listen to people around you. Observation is your best research method for developing a character.

The following are some exercises and processes to help develop and maintain a character.

HIGH STATUS/LOW STATUS

High Status: cool, in control, authoritative, associated with power. Low Status: warm, vulnerable, insecure, powerless.

This is a method of beginning to develop a character from the outside in.

For high status stand perfectly still—don't move a foot, finger and especially your head. Stand erect, chin up and if you remain absolutely still you will find that whatever words you speak will come across with authority and command. A director can call out, "Higher status please" and the actor's character will immediately transform. If you must move, do so very slowly remembering that the tiniest movement will lower your status.

Low status is all about movement—head, arms, whole body as you speak. You will find that the character becomes warm, vulnerable and accessible—not authoritative.

Most characters will have a leaning to either high or low status but no character will be in either status all the time. This is because as humans we find ourselves going from high to low and in-between depending on how we are affected by and respond to the world around us.

MOMENT BEFORE

This is an essential technique to use before going on stage for each entrance in order to be fully in character. How often have we heard an audience member say, "Well, she was very good once she got into it"? We want to be "into it" the moment we step into view.

Before entering, enact in your head, a full 60-second minute of the life of your character just before his/her entrance. If the character is late for an appointment imagine him running to get there along with the thoughts running through his mind. If the character has been summoned think through her anxiety and fears of what is going to happen. If the character is being reunited with a loved one go through the thoughts of anticipation. If the moment before is a full moment and is done in detail, you will enter fully in character and be believable.

Having got on stage in character it is just as important to maintain the character. This requires focus. A character's focus is always connected to what the character wants in that scene. If that focus is maintained, unscripted distractions will be irrelevant.

However, if you do break focus and your mind blanks, breathe. Deep breathing not only relaxes you it also sends extra oxygen to the brain. Most important, while breathing keep your character alive—move, look around with intention but if you are still blank remember it is everyone's responsibility to save the scene, not yours. The poor person who has forgotten the lines is least able to be of help at that moment. Others can incorporate the missing line into a line of their own or improv until the scene is back on track. In a liturgical drama you may be using a narrator who can translate the missing line into narration until things are flowing again. With inexperienced players who

We the Storytellers

are presenting a dramatic story it is a good idea to include a narrator. The narrator has the full text and has the job of reading so the players know they can be saved. This gives the inexperienced players confidence and makes them less nervous.

CHAPTER 6

The Monologue
An Out of Body Experience

A monologue is a one-person performance through a created character developed by an actor.

There are many monologue scripts available in the theater section of bookstores, libraries and on-line.

However, creating your own monologue allows you to express deeply held beliefs or explore and present an aspect of the human condition through a character as actors do in a play. Involving oneself in a monologue is truly an experience of walking in another's shoes, hat and gloves.

Choose a character from the Bible or other literature or from your imagination or personal experience. Use the facts that are known about that character as described in the previous chapter. Add the unknown truths suggested by the known facts using logic and your imagination. You must show us how the character feels, what s/he needs or wants and the close-up details of the situation. Your monologue character will have a setting and theme (a situation, problem or human condition about which you have strong feelings). Allow the character to experience this theme in the monologue. He can talk to the audience/congregation, to himself out loud or to an invisible character on stage. If she is sad, or thrilled, or terrified show us how that emotion presents itself through her senses and body reactions. Use description, metaphor, or dialogue she has with herself. You can also envision the character's surroundings; who and what might s/he encounter, specifically, in the given or chosen setting. If urban there will be vehicles, people, architecture, hard surfaces—in a wooded area there will be animals, trees, other vegetation, and so forth. Showing details of the character's thoughts, feelings and surroundings, with his/her reactions and interactions will bring the listener into the center of your narrative. Remember always to be specific—"a tree" does not create the picture for us that "an old, gnarled elm with her bark peeling away from her trunk" does. And remember that some humor makes us human and so will make your character human too.

Here are two monologues—one an original modern character and the other a biblical character.

This monologue, which I've named, Nice was inspired by a conversation with a young woman searching for her path on a faith journey and by a rereading of Matthew 25. Our conversation followed a production of Talking With . . . , a series of monologues by Jane Martin. This young woman was from the southern United States but could, of course, have been anyone striving to find her relationship with God.

Nice

I'm a Christian but I looove theatre. I go all the time. Sometimes I hear shockin' things and sometimes those things are real funny but, a course, theatre is of the world; it's not religious. Although I heard a person who works in theatre say once, "If a play has somethin' really profound and worthwhile to say then it deserves to be performed—in a theatre, on the street or, maybe the best place, she said, in the church." Well, I wouldn't want any theatre that wasn't about Jesus or that had bad words in it to come into my church. I learned as a child that church is a very special place—a holy place; it's God's house and everthin' in there needs to be clean and proper and nice . . . well especially the people.

Now, when I was a child and I went to church on Easter mornin' in my new shoes and my straw hat and my little white gloves I sat right up front and watched them act out the Easter story. I remember when the women came into the tomb and they looked around and there was no body. Jesus was gone! But the linen clothes were laying there, all rolled up neat, and I knew that could only mean one thang. When Jesus did appear . . . he was gonna be necked. I had to shade my eyes for the rest of the service.

Now I know I was jist a child but still. . . I'm not sure anymore where to find Jesus or what he looks like. Oh I believe, I truly do believe but I feel caught, you know, between the belief of my childhood and what I think I know now. I know God is everywhere; in everthin' yet I cain't think of him, and specially Jesus, in any casual way. I love rip roarin, whoop it up music but I cain't bear to hear Jesus called J.C. or to see him dressed in jeans or some way that isn't. . . nice.

My church did some theatre about folks, you know—characters who I couldn't imagine comin into my church. It was a bunch of monologues; stories about women who made discoveries, I guess, about themselves. Some people who saw the show said the

Gospel was in ever one of those monologues but I couldn't see it. I mean not one of those characters said right out, "I believe in God" or "Jesus is my personal savior." One character, who was a snake handler for the Holiness Church, even said she didn't believe in God anymore said she was able to trance a big ol snake out of a "child's pure love for her father." The monologue went like this:

"Snake, you Satan' handmaiden, you're right there ain't no God in me. I'm just a woman, but I'm the only woman in my dada's house and he needs me home. Outta his faith and his need you lock your jaws."

Well, I don't know what to think about that. (Pause) And another character, lookin' kinda' crazy and dirty like somebody you'd see livin' on the street, said if she had one dream it would be to live in McDonalds mostly 'cus of the plastic. She said,

"God gave us the idea of plastic so we'd know what the everlastin' really was. If there's plastic then there's surely eternity; it's God's hint."

Now I've never talked to anybody livin' on the street but isn't saying that blaspheming?

Course I personally know some of those people who were actin and the characters they played weren't a bit like them. Those people, well the ones I know, are nice, clean, decently dressed and, outside those mono-logues, I never heard any of them say hell or damn, or worse, certainly not in church. People might think that our church is sayin' it's OK to talk and be like that; that God accepts jist anybody.

I read stories and I watch the news on TV and I guess there really are folks like those monologue people in the world—but not in my world. Mind you, sometimes all these pretend characters make me think.

How would Jesus see my life? My world? What would he think of those dirty folks who swear coming into His Church? Surely that's not right, is it? I don't know. I jist don't know anymore . . . but . . . sometimes . . . I can't help thinkin about it and wonderin'—is bein' nice good enough?

And here is a monologue of Mary, the mother of Jesus, that I wrote for the Sunday after Easter Day. We'll call this monologue:

Mysterious Words
(Character wears a long lightweight shawl)
All my life I've held mysterious words in my heart hoping yet fearing that one day I would understand them.

I was young and pretty and naïve. I thought God alone would protect me whatever I did—whatever rules I broke. I felt, as young people so often feel, that my whole life lay ahead of me untroubled and indestructible until those mysterious words and then life, as I knew it, came to an end. I was pregnant.

Those words shot into me like a bolt of lightning, I was thrilled, confused and frightened at the same time—well what young woman isn't faced with the reality of giving birth to her first child. But I. . .(you'll think me foolish now) I truly believed I had been given this life shattering news of unexpected pregnancy by an angel—a terrifying otherworldly being who shone so brightly that I had to turn away and who told me I was chosen by God to bring the savior of human kind into the world.

And there was I thinking I was only a bit late that month!

My cousin, Elizabeth, understood my mixture of emotions. I am so grateful to her for those months together when we could share the experience of creating life in our own bodies.

But I could never have borne the anxiety and sense of awful responsibility without Joseph. He was my teacher my lover and the wise, father of all my children. His understanding and support became the definition of love to me and strengthened me for what was to come. If God is love then, through Joseph, I know God's face.

(Turn in place while sliding stole off and gathering it into a bundle holding it as a swaddled infant)

I still wince with the memory of that unknown fear that laced itself through my joy and gripped me when I first held my infant son. Joseph felt it too; he was so worried that the child and I would not survive the birth in those filthy surroundings—the uncovered, living straw, the smell of animal dung and I saw more than one rat from the corner of my eye.

But when the miracle of birth came, it transcended our surroundings and Joseph and I were awestruck by this perfect tiny human.

As I held him to my breast looking out at the clear dessert sky, the heavens were ablaze with starlight filtering and intensifying my thoughts. Is it possible, I wondered, that my child could be the son of God? What does that mean? And, if it is true, what would this child, my child, have to endure in this world? Salvation has never come cheap. His birth has already drawn interest and rumors and surely those words of prediction will attract enemies. Then I. . .would it mean that I, the mother, must outlive the child? No! I thought . . .

Unimaginable

(Shake off this thought—then on the next line raise the bundle up and gently lay it down nearby)

As he grew I felt such pride for my first born—I favored him I suppose—though really God blessed all my children with just as many gifts as he gave to my first—all my sons and daughters, surely if God is not only beyond us but in us, each birth is a miracle . . . is divine.

But he—he seemed to shine with his own light, well, to his mother anyway. I was silly enough to push him into what would be his short life's work, though if it hadn't been the wine incident at our friend's wedding it would have been something else when he felt ready. Still that was the catalyst for all the glory and all the suffering to come.

And last week during Passover amid the noise of festivity and feasting there was an undercurrent of danger and somehow I sensed, rather than heard, God saying," It is time." And I felt so helpless, so powerless.

Ahh but what would any of us do without our friends and family for support—dear Mary Cleophus, young Magdalene, Peter, and, of course, John—they, who were there for him in his faith and in his doubt. They, through whom I've heard God's voice so many times.

Now—now still reeling from all the horror of little more than a week ago, horror that I would so gladly have taken upon myself to save him that pain, that anguish. . . now, their words, his words, the words fall into place. The words I've held in my heart for so long have meaning at last.

Christ is risen—The Lord is risen indeed. Alleluia!

CHAPTER 7

Silent Eloquence
Mime and Mask

The old expression "A picture is worth a thousand words" comes to mind when I am experiencing a liturgy that is too full of words. We know that body language can communicate volumes of information, especially the emotional state of an individual. Unless we are expert poker players, we will communicate through even our smallest mannerisms and gestures. An actor observes these actions in others and uses them in creating a character.

Words are simply symbols for our thoughts and feelings so using the body's symbolic language makes a refreshing change in communicating ideas in life and in liturgy. We have a variety of traditional gestures that enhance worship for the consecration of the bread and wine, for baptism and the exchange of the Peace. Some liturgies omit verbal instructions entirely which makes for smooth transitions but is hard on visitors. However, most liturgies, in my experience, use more words than necessary which interrupts the flow of worship.

In my story telling classes, at the Toronto School of Theology, I ask the students to divide into groups of three (inherently a balanced visual picture) and create a three minute piece of original wordless liturgy. If they wish, they may use props or fabric and/or sound but no words. When they use simplicity the results can be stunning. One group presented the crucifixion in tableau with a steady background sound of hammering nails. Another three-some portrayed the breath of life with a repeated breath sound and movement that evolved from stillness to full breath and back to stillness representing the Holy Spirit. These pieces need not be scripted—they will emerge quite quickly through the creative process of a small group work-ing together.

Other wordless stories of personal inspiration will come to individuals through blocks of silence (about 3 min-utes) that follow powerful music, poetry or spoken word. And, of course, dance and creative movement have always been a source of "moving" wordless story.

A pleasant deep-toned bell is a useful tool to frame periods of silence.

Some churches use sign language to express elements of their liturgy which is both beautiful to see and inclusive for the hard of hearing.

Actual mime—a story shown without words is akin to dance but with realistic movements and when well done is wonderfully imaginative storytelling. The larger than life, slow motion actions in mime techniques take practice to develop. But once we do, mime is not only a dramatic means of communicating but a relaxing contrast to the fast paced verbal delivery of today's speech. Use some sound, if you wish, but only intentionally. Avoid unintentional grunts or breath sounds.

Try the following exercises alone or with others. After you have developed a sense of the technique, a large mirror is helpful and working with others, for feedback, is even more helpful.

MIME TECHNIQUES

Exercises for Definition

Imagine an object and handle it in mime so that it will be quickly and clearly identified by your audience. Definition may best be achieved by turning a part of the mime performer's body into the object; by holding the object in a definitively characteristic way; by using other imaginary objects in conjunction with it; or by defining a place, a character, or an activity, so closely associated with the object as to identify it at once. For example if the mimed object is a baseball, mime the batter with the bat.

Select a place and identify it in mime. The definition of physical aspects of the place, objects within it, characters frequenting it or activities held there may be required for identification. Example—if the place is the beach, mime laying out the blanket, setting up the umbrella, or putting on lotion, stepping cautiously into the water, and/or enjoying the sensation of walking on sand.

Select a character and identify it in mime. Use a pose, a gesture, a walk, a reaction to an object or a place, a relationship to other characters, or involvement in a particular activity. Any one of these or a combination may be needed to assure recognition.

We the Storytellers

Select an activity, a situation, or an event and identify it in mime.

Mime a series of characters performing the same activity. This can be done by either a number of performers each in a different character or by one performer doing a sequence of characters.

Exercises for Observation

Meticulously observe a person and then mime that person performing some simple activity.

Carefully observe an animal and then mime the animal performing some simple activity.

Exercises for Imagination

Mime an inanimate object—not a character encountering an object, but the object itself. (Something that has inherent movement—an alarm clock, a parking gate, sausages frying).

Select two or three unrelated objects and create a mime in which a character logically encounters them. The logic of the interrelationship is most important. (a roller skate, a remote controlled toy in action, a scatter rug)

Select two totally unrelated activities, events, or situations and create a mime which logically links the two into a cohesive plot. (child misbehaving in car you are driving, man with dog on leash crossing road in front of you reading newspaper as he walks). Imagine the difficulties these two situations can provide, for instance, stop the car and get out to rail at the man—react to honking horns and other drivers shouting at you—while railing at man get caught up in what he is reading in the newspaper while dog runs round and round you wrapping you in his leash—horns and shouting increase—end up by bopping man on the head with his own newspaper and clambering out of the leash. Return to your car only to find that the child is driving it away. As you work on this, more and more details will occur to you.

Exercises for Style

Mime some simple activity. Then try the same activity in super-slow and super-fast tempo.

Mime some simple activity. Then try the same activity set to various contrasting pieces of music. Don't lose the fundamental realism of the mimed activity; mime, don't dance.

Mime some simple activity. Then try the same activity with its movements distorted according to the ground rules of a humanoid group (robots, marionettes, wind-up dolls, fun-house mirror reflections)

MASK WORK

Another way to develop mime technique is through a plain, white, unembellished mask that symbolizes the "every-person." Creating such a mask and wearing it while working on some of the exercises above helps us to recognize and capture our basic human characteristics. The every-person mask assists us to strip our personal habits and acquired characteristics down to our fundamentals. In order for this to work it is better to create our mask rather than buy one and to always treat our mask with respect—even deference because it represents basic humanity.

In performance a plain, white mask continues to present that basic human character and gives the mimist a compelling appearance especially when dressed in black, white, or symbolic color.

The mask can be white make up but a removable mask will obviously free you from your mime role more quickly. One effective and highly personal mask is made from plaster bandage—created on the mimist's own face by someone else. (See illustration 1) It is a messy process and also a trust exercise because the mask maker has control over the model's face and breath!

Plaster Mask Making tools and Materials

An average adult mask will need 2 to 3 roles of plaster bandage (available from a surgical supplier)

You will also need: scissors, Vaseline, a large bowl of warm water, bobby pins and/or a hair band to keep the model's hair out of the way, a towel or cloth to wipe away drips from eyes, mouth or neck of model. And you will need an awl, fine elastic, a tray to set the damp finished mask on and either baby powder or white permanent paint. Both model and maker should wear washable clothes and work in a space that is easy to clean up.

Procedure

Cut a role of bandages into 2 or 3-inch long strips the width of the bandage—you will also need some very slender strips for the upper lip and between the nostrils. These will get you started but you will need to continue cutting strips as you go along.

The model may lie on the floor or on a long table or sit in a chair next to the worktable with a towel around the neck.

Pin back the model's hair and cover every bit of his/ her face, except the eyelids, with Vaseline including the lips and under the chin. Apply plenty of Vaseline to the eyebrows and hairline to avoid pain when removing the mask!

Fill the bowl with warm water and dip a strip of bandage into it squeezing gently just to remove excess water and lay it smoothly on the face. Cover the entire face including mouth and under the jaw over lapping each strip until the face is covered—smooth the strips as you go. Then go back to where you started on the face and apply a second coat covering the seams/joins where ever possible—and then a third coat. Be careful around the eyes; be ready to dab at drips, but get as close as you can; this area will be trimmed later. Be sure that the small, weak areas, between the nostrils and over the upper lip are well coated with bandage but keep the nostrils open!

This material dries quickly so when you think the mask is finished wait only a few minutes and then gently (especially around the hair line) and carefully remove the mask and set it on the tray. If you remove it too soon, it may collapse in places—too late and it is difficult to get off the face.

Immediately poke a hole, with the awl, through each temple where the elastic will go later and for a smoother finish sprinkle baby powder liberally over the mask unless you wish to paint it after it dries.

Clean up!

Allow the mask at least a couple of days to thoroughly dry and then trim off the rough edges all around the face and around the eyes. Wipe off the Vaseline from the inside as thoroughly as possible with a dry cloth or paper towel. Paint if you want to.

Measure the model's head for the length of elastic and tie it into the pre-punched holes.

The model now has a highly personal mask. If treated like every-person masks should be treated, it will last for years.

For performing in mime, with or without a mask, you will need to develop a script which will be a highly detailed description of every action in your silent tale. I've written a sample mime script here.

The Choir Diva and The Fly
(Perform alone and without props, with or without music. Using actual music will require more rehearsal to coordinate sound and action but should be very effective. In either case continual singing in mime is essential.)

The Diva enters as though this were the moment everyone in the audience had been waiting for. She plants herself in the first row of the imagined choir elbowing the invisible choristers to give herself plenty of room. She opens her invisible music folder and nods her head in time to the opening chords of the music; then begins to sing, in mime, animatedly. She reacts to the other choristers around her who obviously prefer a more sedate choral style and want her to do likewise. She ignores their looks and gestures of restraint and sings all the more lustily moving her body in time to the music.

The Diva waves away a pesky fly buzzing around her face. As she continues to sing and move in time to the music the fly stays with her landing on her shoulder, her arm, her head and buzzing all around her. She bats at it in the air with her music folder hitting a few of the other choristers in the process—they hit back. The fly continues to plague her so she moves out of the choir to stalk it. She creeps up on it all the time continuing to sing and move to the music. She punctuates the music from time to time by bashing furiously at the fly sometimes stamping on it when she thinks she has knocked it to the floor. Suddenly, she stops moving but continues to sing. She sees the fly which she follows with her eyes until it lands nearby. She reaches through her choir robe into her pocket and pulls out an invisible revolver, aims at the fly, and shoots. She waits a beat, still singing—no fly. She looks from right to left, up and down—no fly. So, continuing to sing and realizing the big musical moment is coming she moves down center with arms outstretched, head up, and with mouth open wide she sings the final gloriously sustained note. She realizes the fly has flown into her open mouth. She reaches for her throat, then pats her hand slowly down to her stomach moving her body now in rhythm to the fly's movements inside her. Being the consummate professional diva she is, she remembers the audience and smiles, curtsies and blows kisses as she exits still moving in step with the tickly, internal flight of the fly.

CHAPTER 8

Dramatic Space, Fabric, and Lighting

SPACE AND LEVELS

A performance space needs to have levels for visual interest and sometimes for symbolism so take advantage of pulpits, balconies and chancel steps. The pulpit is often a good place to put a high status character—gathering around the altar is often appropriate for making a Eucharistic connection or a scene of a meal and symbolically works well as the Easter tomb. If your scene has to do with baptismal ministry try placing it around the font. If children are involved and height is needed, rather than setting up platforms ahead of time which may get in the way or interrupt the flow of the liturgy, give each child a sturdy plastic milk box. Most grocery stores will sell them to their customers at cost. The child can carry one into position, set it down, and step up on it and then take it away when exiting.

If the space is a chancel and nave it will not be designed for a variety of performances but view it positively. Move your drama or story into the nave. Scenes in the nave create an intimacy by putting the congregation in the center of the action, giving them the role of crowd or community. Remember if you are entering from a pew or elsewhere in the nave, put yourself in character from the second you are seen or heard. Do not walk to the front and then start acting.

Consider the "who, where and what" of your character and how your character is feeling and create clearly audible improvisational lines as you move through the nave and into position for your first scripted line. This same technique can be used for a group or an individual's entrance and can also be used to exit. If it is a group entrance decide on a specific improv. line to say loudly as a cue for the first scripted line.

THE MIRACLE OF FABRIC

I don't sew. I don't even mend but I love fabric.

I've always felt that a worship service should flow, one piece of liturgy inspiring the next so that players and congregation experience a prayerful whole. Therefore, when drama is introduced it needs to become an integral piece of the overall service. I find tightly woven and lightweight fabric provides the perfect set piece or effect for liturgical drama—able to flow, slide or billow its way in, out, and through the worship. Any theatre production be it liturgical, stage, or street will benefit from flow in its staging.

The fabric to look for is lining fabric or, ideally, fabric that is used to make Indian Saris. If it has a metallic thread running through it, it is especially effective as it picks up light beautifully. I use a length of fabric, three yards to six yards long, with a person at either end of the extended fabric holding its' corners. It is best if these persons are of similar height. They gently raise the fabric up and down in great billows or shimmer it at waist height to create the waters of Babylon or the parting of the Red Sea. The longer the arms of the operators the higher the fabric will rise. It is always best to allow the operators to experiment with the fabric, get the feel of it and find out for themselves what it can do before directing specific action. Long lengths of fabric can be used across the chancel or down the aisles; its ability to rise to great heights enables it to be seen anywhere in the space. You can simply buy the fabric and use it as is or for greater control in handling you can hem the ends and slip in a piece of dowel (available at most hardware stores).

I have used a six-yard piece of red satin material, slung over an actor's shoulder as he slowly walks up the center aisle, to represent Simon carrying the cross.

And red fabric brought to life by two operators, during the reading on Pentecost creates an effective background and mood.

The story of Creation in Genesis affords wonderful opportunities for symbolic interpretation by moving various colors of fabric at appropriate points during this long but poetic scripture.

If you have many enthusiastic players it is effective to surround the congregation with billowing lengths of blue and green fabric during the dramatization of Jonah putting the congregation in the center of the storm.

And a lovely bit of magic can happen if, in your Christmas drama, Mary wears a piece of fabric draped over her head or shoulders, extending to her ankles as the shawl for her costume so that at the time of the birth she can slip the fabric down from one side slowly gathering it all into her arms and cradling it like an infant. This takes practice so that the holy birth occurs on "stage" for all to see.

While on the subject of fabric used for costumes I recommend a very simple all-purpose robe style costume design. It is a basic theatre piece and I'm afraid it does require a tiny bit of sewing. For an adult wearer you will need two to three yards of any wide as possible fabric. Depending on the desired length of the cloak either the width or the length of the fabric will ultimately be the length of the garment. Lay the fabric out flat and fold the width or length in half. At the center of the bottom (away from the fold) cut the top layer of the folded fabric from the bottom straight up to the fold and cut a scoop to right and left for the neck. This is the opening of the cloak. Pin and sew three two to four inch wide tucks at either side of the neck opening along the fold (shoulders). Then sew the sides closed from the bottom leaving an ample opening at the top fold for the arms. You may wish to hem the edges without a selvage.

You can also skip the first cut up the center and just cut out a neck opening at the center of the fold for an over the head garment.

Fabric can also be used as a dramatic prop. A long three to four inch wide strip attached to a piece of dowel will make what I call a twirler. Most tight weave fabric of the sort we have been discussing will not fray when torn off or when in use. Start a hole at the end of the dowel with an awl, squirt a little white glue into the hole and twist a small screw eye tightly into the hole. Tie one end of the strip of fabric to the screw eye with strong twine leaving an inch or two of slack. This will keep the fabric from twisting around the stick as the operator holds the stick aloft and twirls it. Twirlers extend the human body up into space and take the focus off the human body when self-consciousness dictates.

They are effective and fun to use in the procession instead of palms on Passion Sunday. On Easter morning I have had an actor create a large vertical circle with the twirler, representing the great stone, and then had the actor keep the circular motion going while she walked slowly sideways. Two or more angels mimed pushing the "stone" away from the tomb. One Christmas a small archangel used a twirler of silver fabric as she made her appearances to accentuate her otherworldly aura.

One more interesting fabric tool is the poi. This is a more effective variation of a twirler without a stick. It requires a cord, a small weight and a short piece of colorful fabric. Pois can be easily made. A student of mine, after being introduced to them in class, made a dozen pois before the next class; she even improved their design! You will need a piece of strong cord a small (about a two inch square) hakki sac or beanbag, a yard length of 4 to 6 inch wide chiffon-like fabric and (for the improvement) a small hook that will snap shut. Permanently attach the cord to one end of the hakki Sac and the hook to the other end of the hakki sac. Punch a grommet or eyelet into the end of the fabric and slip the eyelet over the hook. Make two finger loops at the other end of the cord by attaching rubber washers or loops of leather. Put the middle and fore finger of one hand through the finger loops and practice twirling it until you are comfortable. Then make a second poi for the other hand and work with the two simultaneously. It's easier than it sounds! Because of the hook you can easily change streamers of fabric to have different colors for different occasions. Pois have been used since medieval times and I bought a pair of them at a circus supply shop in London England. If you do not want to make a pair they can, of course, be bought on line. If you order them, specify practice pois as the weights on the non-practice ones are large wooden balls and with them you will knock out half the congregation! They are impressive to use at a celebratory occasion, in a parade or pageant as used traditionally, or as with twirlers they can be used symbolically. I once used a pair of pois to represent the two huge wheels of a cart moving across the stage. The operator bent over from the waist twirling one on each side of him as he walked forward. The "rider" walked behind him waving to the crowds. The possibilities for pois and fabric are endless.

THE LIGHTING

There are occasions when we want to provide an evening performance or liturgy and at those times good lighting is particularly important. In fact, with stained glass windows and typical pendant lights hanging down from a great height, as is the case in many churches, extra lighting may be needed for liturgical drama even in the daytime. My husband, Ernest, in addition to being faithfully perseverant, is a noted lighting designer. He has worked with architects, city planners, government departments and those concerned with light and vision. He has also designed the lighting for many churches and has contributed the following notes on lighting. They are aimed at church people who need enough knowledge to deal with the experts and even do a bit of lighting on their own.

Lighting for Presentations in the Worship Space

Dance and drama as well as music may form part of a service. Moreover, a church may be used for these activities in performance. The following notes assume that the activities take place in an activity space. It could be the chancel, the chancel steps, the center aisle, or a specially designated area. It varies in size from church to church and activity to activity.

If an activity is before a bright window make sure there is good lighting on the actors, even in daytime, otherwise the faces will be dark and without character.

Activity lighting should usually be incorporated easily and unobtrusively into, and form part of, the permanent lighting system. This lighting would use standard commercial luminairs (lighting fixtures) at least fifteen feet above the floor. If you want to be able to dim your lights (much more dramatic than switching on and off) make sure that the system that is being installed is able to be dimmed. Some systems are new and energy saving but cannot be dimmed.

Temporary lighting must be easy to erect and dismantle and not interfere with the church service. Luminaires mounted on stands can be obtained from a theatre supply house. At a pinch reflector lamps with clip on holders can be used on a tall wooden pole mounted in a stand– but with care. Put them out of the aisles or traffic area with sand bags on the bases. Sand bags are also available from a theatre supply house but can be made on an industrial sewing machine by sewing heavy canvas into bags, approximately ten inches square and filling them with sand. If you do not have such a sewing machine take the squares of canvas to a shoe mender to sew.

If an activity is in front of an audience aim the light so that it reaches each part of the activity space from two sides at an angle of forty-five degrees to each side and at an elevation of forty-five degrees (the angle about that of light from a mid-morning summer sun).

If the activity is to be viewed from any direction, the light should come from at least three, but preferably four locations around the space. Screen the lamps from the view of the audience by fitting the luminairs with louvers or barn doors. The latter are hinged flaps fitted at the front of the luminaire.

If the people in the activity space are to be seen, light must shine on them. Give them time to become accustomed to light in their faces otherwise they may look down to avoid it.

The center and side aisles may be used for entrances. Direct a narrow beam of light, a spot, to follow the people making the entrance. This requires someone to operate the follow spot. A follow spot will usually have to be rented from a theatrical supply house and a good place to mount it is on a back balcony rail.

Make sure that your church's electrical circuits will carry the lamp wattage you intend to connect to them. Nothing is more disconcerting than to have the circuit breakers open and plunge the space into darkness. (As I have seen when extra lighting was suddenly switched on for emphasis.)

Safety Measures

- To prevent people from tripping over wires, stick them to the floor with easily removable tape which can be purchased at a theatrical supplier. Duct tape (from a hardware store) can also be used.

- Keep luminairs away from draperies.

- Electrically isolate any electrical device while working on it.

- Do not switch dimmers on and off unless the dimmer settings are "off."

- Keep drinks and water away from all electrical devices.

Lighting for Preaching and Reading

The rector of an Anglican church commented to me, "I have taken your advice and aimed light at the pulpit. Now the members of the congregation who are hard of hearing sit in the third row of pews and lip-read."

The population is getting older. Hearing becomes hard. Reading becomes difficult. Hearing aids are available in some churches, however, it is not usually appreciated that people who are somewhat hard of hearing lip-read unconsciously. This enables them to dispense with the hearing aid. Consequently the face of the preacher, reader, and storyteller must be highlighted. Use the activity lighting approach and do not light straight down.

Sight also becomes difficult as we age. This calls for a higher illumenance (light level), bold type, and a good contrast between what is printed and its background. Black characters on purple paper are not easy to read. (When I design the lighting for a church I try to provide an increased illuminance at an area of seating for the older members of the congregation so they can follow the service books). Make sure that there is light on the walls. Dark walls make a dark looking place even if there is enough light elsewhere

Ernest Wotton, FIET, FCIBSE, FIES, FSLL

CHAPTER 9

Puppets
Instant and Larger Than Life

Puppet is the generic term for all types of puppets—marionettes, shadow puppets, hand puppets, rod puppets, or any combinations of these.

Puppets are believed to be the oldest art form as they've been found in Egyptian tombs. They have a magical heritage in many parts of the world; some cultures made sure that their puppet's heads were removable as they believed that puppets could come alive at night and who knew what they might get up to!

Puppetry is both a visual and a performing art and the essence of puppetry is movement. Puppets are just as effective in communicating with adults as they are with children.

I added puppetry to my resume in New York City when I was hired by Susari Marionettes for my trained speaking voice. This company taught me how to manipulate marionettes and I toured with them throughout the

United States for three years. The tours were five months long and we played in almost every state, city, town and hamlet dragging our stage, lights, sound equipment, props, and puppets with us in a van. I was young enough to find it exhilarating rather than exhausting. We played in schools, community centers, and theatres standing high on bridges erected behind and over the puppet stage operating marionettes with 16-foot long strings. Our stage was set up on the venue's larger stage with their curtains pulled in to meet ours—bringing their stage into the scale of our three foot tall "actors." The marionettes were works of art. They were beautifully carved by a Czechoslovakian wood carver, expertly painted, and so well balanced they could almost stand on their own. The puppet studio where the marionettes were made and kept and where we rehearsed was a dilapidated, old shack of a building in lower Manhattan. It was made clear to all the puppeteers that if ever fire broke out, it would be a pleasant bonus if the puppeteers escaped but it was essential that the puppets got out! I was in awe of these movable sculptures and thought all marionettes should be works of art.

Later I worked for Sid and Marty Kroft in San Francisco performing in their very adult production of Les Poupees de Paris where the three foot tall marionettes were modern but just as exquisitely made as the traditional hand carved wooden ones. Sid and Marty's marionettes were covered in dental enamel and weighed 25 pounds each! They were made to be identical miniatures of famous performers. In this show I was a puppeteer only, as the voices were recorded by the full sized twins of the puppets. Imagine what fun it was for Pearl Bailey, Liberace and Dean Martin to come to our show, sit in the audience and watch themselves perform. Every one of Liberace's fingers was strung so that he appeared to actually play the piano. They all came back stage, of course, to see their miniature selves up close.

When Ernest and Chris and I moved to Toronto I started my own puppet company, building a seven-foot by seven-foot stage and creating marionettes to enact some classic fairy tales. I am not a wood carver and know nothing about working with dental enamel. But I had also worked briefly with Jim Henson of Muppet fame and found I could handle foam rubber and Ping-Pong balls with ease. More important, through discovering the art of creating with found objects (described below) I realized that puppets are about expressing ideas and inspiring new thought—like all art puppets do not have to be beautiful.

I'm grateful for the turn of events that introduced me to puppetry. It is a valuable tool for visually expressing ideas too big for an actor or storyteller to handle alone.

Puppets have also been used as a diagnostic tool with those who have experienced trauma. I have worked with disturbed children in creating and performing with puppets while social workers observed and took notes. Children are often able to talk with a puppet when they cannot talk with a human being. Apparently, if a disturbed child cannot talk with a puppet an extreme diagnosis of certain mental illnesses can be made.

Puppets have no limitations in form. They can have any number of heads or arms (or none) and they can fly. They can be any size—literally as tall as the ceiling will allow. The unlimited size of a puppet is particularly useful for visibility in a church where there are usually no actual stages but very high ceilings. There is a potential for puppets in sermons where puppets may never have been considered. I've known clergy who have involved a particular puppet in the sermon from time to time especially when the topic is controversial. Sometimes removing the person from the words is helpful and few people can get angry with a puppet. Puppets can also bring a charm to celebrations and a familiar puppet can become part of the community. Larger than life puppets are wonderful for pageantry purposes—in procession indoors or outdoors they will be an arresting visual focus and hard to forget.

I think puppets are at their best when used as an appropriate contrast along with actors. When directing productions at the Toronto Centre for the Arts I often used puppets as spiritual, other-worldly or non-human characters—for instance the third spirit in Dickens's A Christmas Carol, the Wizard in The Wizard of Oz (both these puppets were life sized and took two puppeteers to operate) or the dragon in C. S. Lewis' Voyage of the Dawn Treader. The dragon puppet was designed like a Chinese parade puppet but made of cloth and foam rubber instead of paper and took 8 bodies to bring to life. (See illustration 4)

INSTANT PUPPETS FROM FOUND OBJECTS

Once we become aware of what makes a puppet "work" we see that puppets can be created on the spot and there are potential puppet materials all around us. Instant puppets are just as compelling in performance and effective in communication as their hand carved or intricately sewn ancestors.

An instant-puppet-making workshop is ideal for an all-age event on a Saturday or whole weekend, and the best source of materials for this is garbage. Families can recycle artistically. Make some puppets yourself, ahead of time, to use to demonstrate possibilities. Have the participants make one particular design or demonstrate many different puppets to give them a jumping off point for their own creativity. Dump the recycled collection out in the middle of the room so that they can choose heads, bodies, arms, etc. As I said before, puppetry is both a visual and a performing art, and puppets come alive through movement. Encourage everyone to remember the all-important need for movement—it would be better to use nylon stocking arms poked through a milk carton body that just hang down when the puppet is not performing than to use a cardboard tube that looks better when static but will not move in performance. Avoid glue as the movement can cause glued pieces to become unstuck. Instead of glue, tie pieces on or together or use brass fasteners, twisters or duct tape.

Anything used for making puppets is actually manufactured for some other purpose. So, In addition to garbage, borrow some of the practical things you use every day. For example, all items with long handles are themselves the structure for a hand puppet often with a built in head. Consider dish mops, cooking spoons, vegetable strainers, tongs, fly swatters, brushes of all kinds. Keep looking.

For a really instant puppet, place a tea towel over your fist and then place your fist inside a coffee mug with its beak like handle facing forward. A great way to liven up the coffee break!

Or use the gloves or mitts your participants have worn that day which would otherwise be wasting their time waiting around in coat pockets. For a head, tuck in all but the index and ring finger, for ears, of one glove, ball up a page of newspaper and put it inside that glove and apply two big stickers for eyes. Then for the body put the other glove on your hand and push your three middle fingers up into the stuffed glove behind the ball of newspaper leaving your little finger and thumb out as puppet arms. All who wore gloves that day have an instant puppet. Those who wore mitts can, of course, adapt this design to have a creature with a tongue or a beak or a tail. You can also buy colored stretchy, one-size-fits-all gloves at most dollar stores or use cotton garden gloves

Because the essence of puppetry is movement, look for things that have a moveable part. For instance scissors can become the jaws of an alligator; hold them with the blades protruding from an old sleeve, sock or pant leg. Or create a head from a jug, ball or box and drive it down on the point of an umbrella. The action of the umbrella will be very effective and depending on the umbrella's design the character can be a large, menacing bird or a ballerina in ruffled, flowered skirt. In the realm of instant puppets, everything becomes a character. In order for their personalities to be seen from a distance, puppets need large heads, eyes and hands out of proportion to their bodies and long, out of scale arms or other features that carry their gestures.

One very effective puppet is made with a plastic jug with handle (detergent, vinegar, etc.) and good-sized piece of fabric around a meter/yard square. The handle side of the jug gives the head a wonderfully dramatic, sculptured face. Remove the screw cap from the jug and place the center of the piece of fabric, good side down and diagonally (to allow for longer arms) over the jug opening and screw the cap back on and turn the jug over. A hand can be a thick cardboard mitt with the "wrist" poked into a fold on the far corner of the right side (if you are right handed) of the fabric. Staple the wrist to the fabric on the under-side. Finish the face with contrasting colored felt marker or cutout circles of colored tape (make the features large) and add a hat if you wish. To operate hold the screwed on top from inside the fabric with one hand and grasp the wrist of the hand inside the fabric with your other hand for gesturing. This style of puppet with its large head and eyes and long arm can be seen from a distance and it has the capacity for more movement because it uses both your hands to operate. It is equally effective in the pulpit or classroom. (See illustrations 2a to 2d for examples of instant puppets)

And Then They Perform

Visible puppeteers are no problem as long as the puppet is held slightly higher and in front of the puppeteer's own head. I often perform with a puppet when I am fully visible to the audience. Once, standing with a puppet in front of children, my puppet listened to the group's description of a trip they had taken. I then produced another puppet and the children began to tell their trip story again from the beginning. Their teacher said to them, "You've already told that story" and they responded, "But we haven't told this puppet." Puppets can tell a story, act as characters in a scripture drama or two or three can improvise on a theme. If the theme involves a problem or conflict the performance can set up an interesting discussion.

They also move well to music and make a charming visual to a song or a story that is narrated. This non-talking style of puppet performance is especially good for inexperienced or shy actors.

PAGEANT STYLE PUPPETS

This style of puppet is appealing to teenagers—perhaps because of its size and consequent need for some height and strength in the operators making it clear that this isn't a children's toy. This style of puppet also generally requires two people to operate.

Here is my design for a larger than life pageant style puppet:

Small Tools and Equipment Needed

Scissors, duct tape, Contact cement, clothes pegs, spray paint, serrated knife, 2 lengths of half inch dowel, your choice of embellishments from a hardware or dollar store.

Materials and Procedure

A piece of foam rubber: at least a yard to six and a half feet square, one to two inches thick. This will be for the head and the hands. You will want the foam to be thick enough to have body and not cave in on itself but not too thick to be flexible. Before experimenting with your head you will need to cut off and set aside enough foam for hands and smaller features such as nose, ears, etc. This thickness of foam can be cut with scissors.

A block of foam rubber: approximately four or five inches square in thickness and approximately eighteen inches long. This is for the shoulders. Foam rubber can be found at shops that sell foam rubber mattresses and if they have scraps, ask for them, as they will always come in handy.

A string floor mop: another long rod like a broom, other style of mop or leaf rake could be used but these directions are for a string mop. You will attach this to the head to operate it with the strings becoming its hair.

A sturdy tube: very heavy cardboard if you can find it—bolts of fabric are sometimes on these tubes and the shops throw them out. If these are not available get a plastic tube used in construction, 6 inches to a few feet long, or the same length piece of drainpipe. It should be strong but reasonably lightweight. This should be large enough in diameter for your mop handle to slip into and move easily and small enough to hold comfortably in your hand. The tube is for moving the shoulders.

A large piece of fabric: as wide as possible and at least two to three yards long. This will be the puppet's body. The fabric needs only to suit the character of the puppet. I once provided an education block for an Anglican General Synod which involved storytellers and a fourteen-foot high puppet, named Ellie, who represented the Earth's elements. The head was fire red, the body a shimmering water blue, the hands and body map-shape details were brown with an air-like flowing action when the puppet moved. (See illustration 3)

Assembly

Determine who or what your puppet is or you may want to create the puppet and decide what it is afterward.

First play with the foam for the head. Take as long as you need arranging the foam in your hands pulling it into different positions. I advise you not to cut it but to leave it whole while you experiment. Clip it in various positions with clothes pegs to see the different looks. When you have the head shape you want, open a window for ventilation and place the head on newspaper. Apply contact cement to both edges that you wish to join, wait a few minutes and then press them firmly together and let the glue dry.

While the glue is drying cut out the large hands from your extra foam using scissors. I recommend mitt style hands, as they are less fragile than hands with fingers. When you cut them include wide, long wrists and wrap these wrists around one end of a length (approximately four feet) of half inch dowel applying duct tape to hold them in place.

Next, make a slice in the precise middle of the block of shoulder foam. Do not cut a hole—make a slice with a knife all the way through the foam—the slit just wide enough to push the tube through, leaving a few inches of tube above the shoulder foam. Wrap duct tape around the tube several times above and below the foam to keep the tube from slipping up or down.

Center the width of the fabric on the shoulder foam. The length of the fabric will be vertical and the width horizontal. The fabric should touch the floor for the front of the puppet when you hold the tube with shoulder piece attached in front of you at approximately your shoulder height. The fabric at the back of the puppet should be shorter than floor length for easier access to tube and rod. When you have the fabric width centered on the puppet's shoulders and the length appropriately distributed cut a slit in the fabric over the top of the tube just wide enough for the tube to slip through. Remove the fabric and apply contact cement to the top of the foam shoulders. Wait a few minutes and then slip the fabric slit over the tube and press the fabric in place smoothly and evenly over the shoulders.

Return to the headpiece and determine the details of the face. Think big especially for the eyes. If you want a nose or ears the best method is to cut out triangle pieces from scrap foam. Make a slit with a knife all the way through the foam head at the points where you want the nose or ears to go. Bring two corners of a triangle piece of foam together and you will see the shape. Poke the bottom of the triangle you are holding, firmly into the slit on the head and it will be sucked in and will stay. So make large triangles, as the base will be submerged. If you want a colored head and hands you must use spray paint. For best results, use the spray paint made for foam.

When the paint is thoroughly dry, make slits with the knife in the top and the bottom of the head just wide enough to push the mop handle into the top of the head and out the bottom and into the shoulder tube. The strings of the mop are now the puppet's hair, left hanging or braided or cut into a style!

Finally, thread fish-line or strong cord through each side of the edge of the front fabric, about half way down and tie this cord around the wrists of your puppet hands, that are attached to rods and your puppet is assembled.

Operation

This puppet will need two puppeteers. One, the body puppeteer, stands behind the puppet with hands inside the fabric to move the body. He/she will hold the tube in one hand, to move the body itself and, when wanted to move the shoulders. This puppeteer will grasp the mop handle below the tube with his/her other hand to turn the head. The other puppeteer stands directly behind the body puppeteer to move the arms holding the ends of the dowel rods.

Needless to say it will take time for the two puppeteers to develop the necessary cooperation with one another which can be a worthwhile action in itself!

Note: Puppeteers are always behind their puppets and therefore the only ones who can never see the puppet in action so feedback is vital and mirrors can be useful. I also suggest positioning the puppet's face exactly forward and taping a coin to the mop handle rod where the puppeteer will place her/his hand. This is to let the puppeteer know when the puppet is facing forward.

CHAPTER 10

Public Reading and Memorization

READING

We now learn to read at an earlier and earlier age but it has been my observation that reading aloud is no longer practiced in most schools and so the confidence in this skill has been lost. As I have said (and said), I do believe that telling a story to an audience is much more effective than reading it. However, there are times when good reading is appropriate in liturgies and on other public occasions. This is especially true when story is not involved as in an epistle or speech or when time is an overriding factor. As people learn to read more and more effectively they go through four stages:

1. Reader's nose in the book/paper never looking up

2. The bobbing method where the reader pops his/her

head up periodically not looking at anyone

3. Reading with a balance of looking at the text and look-
    ing at individual audience members, but rushing the
    eyes back to the text for the last word of a sentence.

4. Reading as in 3 but without needing to rush back for
    those last words.

Tips and Techniques

It is a good idea to enlarge the font of the reading to a comfortable size when holding the text at chest level. Avoid a
flapping paper by placing a file folder or book under it. Run
your finger down the right hand side of your text slowly as
you read so that when returning to your text after looking
up you can easily find your place. This should help you avoid
rushing back for last words. When preparing your reading
underline the dramatic, poetic, or most important words,
phrases or sentences that you particularly want to share
with full eye contact. If you have a tendency to drop your
voice at the end of sentences (a common problem) you can
indicate in your text where you need to take a breath (before you are out of air) so that you can complete a thought
with full energy. You might also underline all subject nouns
and action verbs to remind you to say them clearly. Your
audience can grasp feelings and description from your facial expression and body language but to follow the gist of
what you are reading they must hear the subject and action words. Don't be afraid to pause especially after reading
something that is notable—allow your audience a little time
to digest what they hear. You want to make eye contact with
many people in every direction, but don't stay with one
person so long that it makes him/her uncomfortable. Let
movement of the body and gestures come naturally as they

do in conversation—planned gestures usually come across as contrived. If you take steps, do so with a purpose—avoid pacing and most definitely avoid rocking or swaying from foot to foot. Give your voice color and variety by letting your hearers see and hear your interpretation of the text. Breathe down to the diaphragm for vocal energy and smile!

MEMORIZING

1. Do not memorize words. The actor first memorizes the thought progression of each scene. Memory work must always include scenes as whole units, not isolated lines or speeches.

2. When performing with someone else, memorize cues as well as lines. Again it is more important to know what is happening rather than what is being said.

3. Break down each subdivision or thought change of your text into individual beats (marked in your text with a /. A beat is what you feel is a complete thought. This is to help you, personally, to memorize. There are no definitive beat changes; others might mark beats in the same text differently. Often when starting to memorize a text you will get stuck at a certain spot, this is probably a beat change for you. Title your beats with a phrase containing a central core verb (For instance, "Making a phone call" or "Questioning William about last night"). This will also help you memorize the thought progression of the scene. Some find it helpful to retype script/material making a new paragraph for each beat so that they can visualize each beat more clearly when performing.

4. Some actors find it best to memorize lines without trying to put any emotion or interpretation behind

them. This will help the actor avoid "rehearsing" interpretations which may make your delivery wooden and keep you from thinking about what you are saying. Your interpretations may change and grow as you work on your text.

5. All memory work should strive for eventual word-for-word exactness. Do not allow paraphrasing or ad libbing, even at early off-book rehearsals. It will invariably end up being memorized at some level. (This is a highly subjective statement, but seems proven in practice.) Know that you will have the skills of improvisation to fall back on, if necessary, in performance, as your audience has not seen your script!

6. Memorize lines in a short amount of time—never more than a week. Set deadlines and keep them. Long rehearsal periods of "getting off books" results in an uneven finished product and large gaps in character development.

7. I find memorizing a text in chunks or paragraphs helpful. A paragraph may include more than one beat. Learn paragraph one then two then one and two together then three then one, two, three together and so forth. This gives me confidence that I am progressing with the memorization of the text.

8. In your final stages of rehearsing do it on your feet and out loud. Some actors find it helpful to rehearse in different spaces so as not to become reliant on visual cues in the rehearsal space unless the rehearsal space is also the performance space.

Most important when presenting memorized material—keep breathing deeply. This literally helps the memory by feeding increased oxygen to the brain. And while breathing keep your body "alive"—move, use pause as if you intend it and focus on what is happening in your story or monologue until the words return (and they will!)

CHAPTER 11

Story Writing
The Basics

This chapter is a writing workshop focusing on techniques of writing. I will try to provide an overview of the essential elements in writing fiction and personal stories and include some exercises for you to do independently. My hope is that the stories in Part 1 will give you a jumping off point to write your own sacred stories.

The hardest part of writing for many is where to start. So we will start there with the possible structures or shapes of a story. Stories do not have to be chronological but they need to have a beginning, a middle and an end. Their beginnings should draw the reader/listener in, keen to read more. Your central character will always want something strongly just as on stage and in life. What this character wants will drive your story. And conflict in a story is essential. So you could start with an event that involves conflict—interior or exterior ("That's Bob's car in front of the house, I'm sure it is. He knows the restraining order doesn't allow him to get that close. Well, if he doesn't know now he soon will!"). Or an opening may involve unknown facts ("After my experience yesterday and the way they reacted I'm ready for this trip now." What experience? How did they react? What trip?) We keep reading to find out what will happen or what the writer knows that we don't. The writer must then introduce more characters through scenes with dialogue and narration always painting a picture of people and places, very specifically. "A dog" doesn't give us a picture, "a cocker spaniel wagging his tail in greeting" does. Writing, like acting, is showing not telling. The reader wants to share the experiences of a story with the writer not just be told about it. Dialogue is an excellent way to provide description and to show rather than tell through what one character says to or about another so bring dialogue in early and frequently. While creating these scenes remember to focus on what your main character wants and let it drive your story right to the story's climax or conclusion. Your narration presents a point of view and must remain consistent. This is an opportunity for you to say something important or worthwhile through your story. Always include conflict, interior or exterior, in your story to make it real and to keep the story line alive. Then after the climax, comes the denouement. This is more than an ending; it is what makes your story make sense. Some stories tie up neatly, some have an open ending that leaves the reader with questions to ponder, others are circular and repeat the opening lines or phrase at the end with a meaning that shows the main character's growth. But whatever your ending it is an important piece and you will need to reread your story many times to find just the right resonating words and phrases.

So to sum-up:

- You need to "hook" your reader at the beginning

- Know what your main character wants and focus on it throughout your scenes.

- As the narrator, be consistent in your point of view.

- Use plenty of dialogue and be specific in description— show don't tell!

- Create a denouement that provides full understanding of your story.

And to add to this, a few words about Plot Designs and about language:

When designing a profluent (forward moving) plot writers work in one of three ways—sometimes two or more at once. The writer borrows some traditional story or action from life or literature and writes a story based on this or creates a story entirely from imagination and then, works backward from his/her climax or works forward from an initial situation

In language, words from Latin origin are descriptive even poetic and often create the moments that we remember as the lovely part of a story. Anglo-Saxon words are the ones to use when we want to speak plainly and directly and when we need strength in our language.

NOTES ON DENOUEMENT

A denouement is not simply the end of the story but the story's fulfillment. The reader now understands everything and everything is symbolic.

Unfortunately, a good denouement cannot be taught and is probably impossible to anticipate in the planning of your story. Perhaps the most useful suggestion is to read the story at least 100 times, literally. Watch for subtle meanings, connections, accidental repetitions, psychological significance. Leave nothing unexamined and when you discover implications in some image or event nudge those implications toward the surface. This may be done by introducing subtle repetitions of the image, so that it catches the reader's subliminal attention; by slipping the image into a metaphor that helps to fix and clarify the meaning you have found in it; or by placing the image (or event or whatever) in closer proximity to related symbols.

Two warnings: Don't overdo the denouement by pushing meaning which can give the narrative a too conscious, contrived, workshop effect and don't, on the other hand, write so subtly or timidly, out of fear of sentimentality or obviousness that no one notices the dénouement.

If your story is being used as a drama in liturgy and you have a large number of enthusiastic players look for characters that are not specified. For instance, if you are dramatizing the Christmas story you know that Bethlehem was crowded, "No room at the Inn." So you can begin with many players entering with improvised lines creating a crowd to set the scene of the story. Or if your story takes place in the forest, there is an opportunity to create scenes featuring nonhuman creature characters. When presenting your dramatisation of a biblical or other story from literature read between the lines and let the setting provide additional characters. Conversely if there are few players involved, cast and feature the main characters with actors and allow a narrator to carry the rest of the story.

Here is a full list of notes for you to use when creating and editing your stories.

WRITER'S CHECK LIST

- Point of view—narrator's position on story
- Show! don't tell (especially when describing how a character thinks or feels)
- What does the protagonist (main character) want?
- Establish the who, where, what, when and why
- Use strong nouns and verbs (don't rely on adverbs & adjectives)
- Limit repetition of words (unless using for effect)
- Balance sentence lengths
- Specificity in description of character, time & place
- Clarity and precision of language
- Creative metaphors (avoid clichés)
- Humor makes a story human and therefore believable
- Smooth paragraph transitions
- Dramatize with dialogue and scenes
- Conflict is human and holds the reader's attention—it is essential for story energy
- Focus on driving the storyline with what the protagonist wants
- Consistent style of language for narration (Latinate/ high/ archaic—Anglo-Saxon/plain/ strong)
- Consistent tense
- Knowledge and feeling for subject
- Punctuation for Reader Guidance
- Balance of narration and dialogue

- Write hot (get it all out), edit cool (Cut unnecessary words)
- Spell check!

If submitting use standard 7 point check list unless otherwise specified (spell check, indent paragraphs, double space, Times New Roman font, 12 point font, number the pages, identify each page with your name or story title)

EXERCISES

1 The Opening: Establishing Main Character

Write a first page, double-spaced, involving a person (different from you in 3 significant ways) who is in the process of going to another country or city for a reason—to accomplish something important to him or her.

This will develop into an evolving story in third person encompassing a who, what, when, where and why.

Question the use of every adjective and adverb. Are you using them because you have not found the right noun or verb?

Use metaphors and similes but avoid clichés!

Describe your character indirectly through her impact on others—the way they respond to her and be aware of all senses not just visual. Write hot, edit cool. Go big you can always cut back.

Be as specific as you can be.

Keep whole story moving forward to a purpose.

Show physically how characters feel emotionally—limit summary narrative, show, don't tell—show through action, gestures, posture, senses and dialogue. People reveal themselves through action. Static description doesn't work as well as motion. Characters must respond to what happens to them.

2 Description and Point of View

Write a descriptive passage, in your evolving story, up to two pages (double-spaced) max. Your main character has now arrived.

Describe character involved in action—revealing her/himself in action—not static description. Establish point of view. Writer, as narrator, is outside character and describing from a distance like a camera.

Check adjectives and adverbs. Let reader see and figure out what character is doing—don't tell them how the character feels.

Get order of action right, in succession especially if going back in time and returning to present.

3 Conflict and Dialogue

Character encounters another character who is bent on thwarting your character's main intention. Use conflict in dialogue. Remember conflict can be interior as well as exterior. Write three pages double-spaced max.

In dialogue bury the "s/he saids" or other tag lines in the midst of the dialogue rather than dangling them at the end. Characters must respond to one another. Dialogue is like ping pong or tennis. Use echoes and conflict and obstacles. We learn about characters through their disagreements. This is where they reveal themselves.

Lay out dialogue with each character's line(s) a separate paragraph. Use dialogue as much as possible. It is great for revelation of character although not as good for expository information. So go back and forth between dialogue and narration. Indirect dialogue is summing up what character is saying.

Capture character's distinctive diction rather than phonetic rendering of dialect. One character cutting off another is shown like this: "_____." For pause or trail off use: . . . You can do without the "he/she saids" by making each character clear through the character's choice of vocabulary and context.

4 Characters and Scenes to Climax

Write 4 pages double-spaced max.

Imagine the climax. Stay with your story line above and decide what characters are needed to arrive at the climax and what they are like. Sketch their biographies for yourself—name, age, physical description, personality type, profession, likes and dislikes, background and use this information to create the remaining scenes that culminate with the climax. Then read, reread and reread your story to find your perfect finish!

CHAPTER 12

Brief History of Sacred Drama

A Chapter of the Church's Story

The evidence of art (paintings, hangings and sculpture/ icons) show us that for almost a thousand years the church was symbolized by depictions of paradise which was seen to begin here on Earth. The cross and crucifix are not found as symbols of the church until the nine hundreds or the time of the "holy wars." I find this an interesting period of the church's story especially for its political ramifications. For those who are interested in this aspect of the first ten centuries of the church's history I recommend the book Saving Paradise: How Christianity Traded Love of This World for Crucifixion and Empire by Rita Nakashima Brock and Rebecca Ann Parker.

However, as this is a brief history it will begin in England with the Middle Ages and the Mystery Cycle Plays, series of plays that depicted the history of the world from a Christian perspective.

Traditionally, the Mystery Plays were performed at Corpus Christi, a major religious holiday that took place in mid-summer and was as important in medieval times as Christmas is today.

English society was deeply religious at that time and the Mystery Plays were an excellent means of communicating tales from the Bible to the masses, many of whom could not read at all, and could not understand Latin, the language of the liturgy. The York Cycle has fifty plays in total (perhaps the longest original Cycle) and fifty ornate wagons filled with actors and singers were pushed and pulled through the streets by teams of men. They stopped at designated places, known as stations. Most of the original Cycles were done in this way, telling the stories from Creation to The Last Judgment. By the close of the fourteenth century York had twelve stations. Fifty plays performed 12 times made for a long day! Even starting at four thirty a.m. they didn't finish until mid-night by the light of torches.

In Medieval English the word "mystery" means a "craft" and the Mystery Plays were so called because each play was presented by one of the city's craft guilds. Different guilds often presented highly appropriate stories, for example, the shipwrights were responsible for 'the building of the Ark' while the butchers played 'the death of Christ.' This tradition has continued in recent revivals. In two thousand and two in York, for example, 'the creation of the world' was presented by The York Guild of Building.

Few medieval towns could afford to do plays so fully and elaborately and original texts survive from only five English cities—Chester being the most complete in existence. Chester's Cycle was also the longest running as it was the last place to succumb to an ecclesiastical ban in the fifteen hundreds.

Today, after a break of over four hundred years, the original Cycles are presented every few years in Chester and occasionally in York and a few other towns in England. New productions are also springing up like the Passion I saw in Oxford and the Gosforth Mysteries outside Newcastle in two thousand and seven.

In the nineteen eighties Tony Harrison adapted the medieval texts for the National Theatre in London, England. This production inspired an American adaptation for the American Court Theatre in Chicago in the nineteen nineties.

Each production, ancient and modern, is staged in different creative ways each time it is produced. Most of the actors are keen amateurs who live and work in the community where the plays are presented and most of the directors are professionals which follows the original intent while at the same time produces a quality production.

The direction and staging does more than simply tell the stories—they also present a point of view. The notes from the director of the Chester Mysteries staged in two thousand and eight, list among the ten 'Design Requirements' the following: ". . . Christianity is built on a foundation of earlier religions—from which Christianity takes ideas, symbols, and theology—therefore the base of the set will comprise of ruins of pre-Christian religions. And Hell will be partly visible—like a plague spreading throughout the set. Also, to intensify the real/unreal characters and scenes the design of both set and costumes will emphasize the overblown surreal aspect of their characters. For example, the Pharisees will wear out-of-proportion robes and block shoes. Pilot will be in an exaggerated cloak to represent the domination and size of influence of the Roman

Empire. This will contrast with Christ's Passion and the simplicity of his environment and followers."

In Canada, the University of Toronto's Medieval Studies Department mounts one of the original Mystery Cycles every few years with groups from all over Canada and the United States and even some from England participating. I sense an increased interest in plays of this sort (or perhaps it's just the company I keep!)

While no longer illiterate we are becoming increasingly untutored in the biblical stories so if Mystery Cycle productions are on the rise they may be as true to their original purpose as they were in medieval times.

In addition to the Cycle plays, religious drama in general went through that long period when it was viewed with antagonism in the church and suspicion in the theatre. Some may still view the arts in those ways. In fact, it was as recent as nineteen twenty-eight that the first play was performed in an English cathedral since the Reformation. The cathedral was Canterbury and the play was the Nativity. The drama of the medieval Christian church had begun with the Resurrection and the Incarnation. It was appropriate after centuries of banishment that theatre return with a traditional play. And in nineteen fifty one a selection of plays from the York Cycle was produced for the Festival of Britain with a teenaged Judi Dench playing the part of an angel.

In the nineteen thirties, T.S. Eliot was commissioned to write a new play for the Canterbury Festival; it was Murder in the Cathedral. This play broke the historical mold while at the same time it used the most ancient form of drama—the liturgical.

With Murder in the Cathedral, modern religious drama entered the professional theatre. Authors such as

Charles Williams, Dorothy Sayers, Christopher Fry and many others followed Eliot's lead.

Then came World War Two and the ministry of drama was urgently needed as it provided entertainment, hope and comfort to many. These wartime companies made history both in the theatre and the church. The theatre of direct contact with the audience, of an experience shared rather than viewed, has gone on growing from those roots.

By producing drama in the church I was, in my small way, contributing to the movement of bringing theatre home. Drama and storytelling have always fascinated me. As a young teenager I chose to go to church on Sunday morning while my mother slept in—there's a role reversal for you. We were High-Church Episcopalians and I thought the "show" was terrific. Frankly, I still do. The use of symbols and symbolic gestures and the sense of mystery in this style of worship is, for me, a moving and inspirational experience. I knew from the age of ten that I would make theatre my profession. I think from the beginning, my leaning to the performing arts and my Anglo-Catholic proclivities influenced each other and quite naturally came together. One does not, however, need to have smells and bells to use the arts effectively in worship. The arts are a language that is able to serve all forms and styles of worship. The arts also record the church's history through music, wall paintings, icons, poetry and prose.

There is no longer a division between religious and secular drama. The insights of an author may prove religious no matter what the outward form of their expression. A playwright becomes in a dramatic moment a theologian—a person of faith taking a venturesome look into the unknown.

Further Reading

THEATRE AND THE ARTS

Audition by Michael Shurtleff

Building A Character by Constantin Stanislavski

Creating Change: The Arts as Catalyst for Spiritual Transformation by Keri K. Wehlander

Dancing On the Ark by Kelly Walker

Freeing the Natural Voice by Kristin Linklater

Impro: Improvisation and the Theatre by Keith Johnstone

Improvisation for The Theatre by Viola Spolin

Staging The Story: new plays for worship and church gatherings by Sally Armour Wotton

Strange Angels and Other Plays by Scott Douglas

Theatre Games by Clive Barker

The Mysteries Part One: The Creation, and Part Two: The Passion by Edward Kemp for the Royal Shakespeare Company

The Mysteries: The Passion (One of a series) by Nicholas Rudall and Bernard Sahlins

Walking on Water: Reflections on Faith and Art by Madeleine L'Engle

STORY

Story Theology by Terrence W. Tilley

Tell Me Another by Bob Barton

Tell Us Our Names: Story Theology from an Asian Perspective by C.S. Song

The Song of The Bird by Anthony de Mello

The Way Of The Storyteller by Ruth Sawyer

Any book on story theology by William Bausch, E.B. White, John Shea or Joseph Juknialis

MONOLOGUE:

American Dreams: Lost & Found, or Working by Studs Terkel

Audition!—A complete Guide for Actors by Joan Finchley

Encounters at Bethlehem by Jean Jones Andersen

Monologues: Women and Monologues: Women 2 and Monologues: Men by Robert Emerson & Jane Grumbach

Talking with . . . by Jane Martin

Any of the many *Scenes for Student Actors* books

WRITING

Bird by Bird by Anne LaMott

The Art of Fiction by John Gardner

The Broadview Guide To Writing by Doug Babington and Don LePan

PUPPETRY

German Puppet Theatre Today by Hans R. Purschke

Making Shadow Puppets, Search Press London, Herder and Herder New York

My Profession by Sergei Obraztsov

Puppetry in Canada: An Art To Enchant by Kenneth B. McKay with photography by Andrew Oxenbam

Puppetry Today: Designing and making marionettes, glove puppets, rod puppets and shadow puppets by Helen Binyon

Synopsis

We the Storytellers provides examples and techniques for expressing deeply held beliefs through the oldest form of communication—stories. This book can be used as a resource on narrative theology for preachers, teachers, and storytellers.

Narrative theology is about pealing back the known to discover the unknown. Rather than pronouncing facts it gives an opportunity for an "ah ha" experience. In a sermon it allows the hearer to grasp an element of truth through fiction or personal story—Jesus's method. And narrative theology is about revealing the relationship between God and God's people. What better way to look at relationships than through stories?

The book is written in two parts. Part 1 asks the question, what is a sacred story and offers a number of possibilities. Part 2 is a workshop on acting, writing, and presentation skills aimed at those who are drawn to expressing themselves through stories.

The stories here are from Sally's own life experiences—the monologues from her imagination. Each story is related to a theme and is humorous, poignant and human.

The hope is that We The Storytellers will inspire and equip its readers to develop and perform their own sacred stories.

Author Biography

Sally Armour Wotton trained and worked in the New York City theatre. In Toronto Canada she formed Sacred Acts with Alexandra Caverly Lowery, dancer, and Kelly Walker, musician. This company facilitated events in the performing arts across Canada.

Her previous book, Staging The Story, is widely used as a resource in liturgical drama. Sally teaches courses on storytelling and story writing in the faculty of Trinity College, School of Divinity, University of Toronto.